RE/DEFINE TRADITION

ARCHITECTURE CHINA

CONTENTS

RE/DEFINE Tradition

Li Xiangning
Editor-in-chief, Architecture China
Professor, College of Architecture and Urban Planning,
Tongji University

Urban construction in contemporary China has experienced 30 years of continuous development. While it created an evolution pattern in the built environment unseen in the West, it may have also severed the connection between the architecture of Chinese cities from a more traditional world, to a certain degree. The decorative and structural systems that follow a characteristic Chinese order or the exemplary *dougong* (interlocking wooden brackets) covered by a vast roof seem to have lost their resonance with the pulse of the zeitgeist and modern society.

The challenges are self-evident. On one hand, the Chinese architectural circle is struggling to make up for the lessons of modernity from the West. On the other hand, it is lamenting the rapid disappearance of its own cultural tradition. How to self-locate within the coordinates of East-West and tradition-modernity is the ultimate question that every Chinese architect must answer. Outside the academic world, attention has also been paid to the issue of tradition at a national level. The 2017 changes and additions to the Constitution of the Communist Party of China clearly state that it shall strive to develop educational, scientific, and cultural undertakings, and "promote the creative evolution and innovative development of fine traditional Chinese culture." From the perspective of architectural culture, this phrase allows for a wide range of interpretations.

Architecture China Winter 2019 presents answers to this essential question from 16 architects. Among them, some try to tap the potential of traditional architectural forms and structural systems with contemporary formal language; some use traditional building types as a basis to create new spaces that respond to the needs of contemporary life; and some focus on the application and innovation of traditional materials. If the above-mentioned practices respond mostly to tradition in the sense of classical Chinese architecture, other architects have expanded the discussion by including the recent collective memory and the globalized traditions of others. Ultimately, these 16 architects re/define tradition with their unique answers, while also inspiring a different understanding of the concept.

Vitalization of building techniques and crafts

Timber structures are one of the most iconic characteristics in the tradition of Chinese construction. The overlapping columns, beams, purlins, and lintels form the typical modular open spaces. The layered *dougong* support the roof with low eaves and slightly raised corners, while the microscopic mortise and tenon joints form a delicate and poetic connection between the different structural components. Following the popularization of modern construction technologies centered on a Tetris-like frame system and reinforced concrete, the construction of traditional timber structures has seen a steady decline due to their inability to meet the structural and fire safety requirements of modern spaces. But in recent years, timber construction has regained the attention of contemporary architecture, which is undoubtedly influenced by the demand for low-carbon development of buildings and cities. Yet more important for this phenomenon are the efforts of Chinese architects to find a connection to China's lost construction tradition.

In the central Chinese province of Hunan, academician Chang Qing designed Quzi Academy using a vernacular *chuan-dou* woodwork structure with columns, purlins, and lintels to form a bidirectional woven frame. As a place to commemorate the famous ancient poet Qu Yuan, the timber structure recreates the ritual memory of the buildings of the poet's time by dividing the space into an even number of sections by a central row of columns. Similarly, in the ruins of Pan Village's ancestral temple in nearby Anhui Province, Wang Hao reinterpreted the local timber construction tradition by merging it with contemporary techniques. To do this, he combined the traditional *chuan-dou* with a Western steel-and-wood structure and a new mortise and tenon joint called "bundled columns with stacked beams."

Typological reinterpretation

Aldo Rossi wrote in *The Architecture of the City* (1966) that "the concept of thus became the basis of architecture, a fact attested to both by practice and by the treatises." He stated further: "Type is a constant and manifests itself with a character of necessity; but even though it is predetermined, it reacts dialectically with technique, function, and style, as well as with both the collective character and the individual moment of the architectural artifact." Just as types are related to specific spatial forms and lifestyles in a certain period, they constitute a cultural continuity that crosses the dimensions of time, thus becoming a connection between the past and the present.

Courtyards are perhaps the most common spatial type in traditional Chinese dwellings. Both Studio Zhu-Pei's Shou County Culture and Art Center and Neri&Hu's Tsingpu Yangzhou Retreat were borne out of the reinterpretation of the courtyard concept. The former is based on the characteristic vertical courtyard, and the thick walls and small windows of Huizhou folk houses. The project reshapes the spatial experience of these folk houses from central room to back garden with inward-facing courtyards. A winding and undulating corridor connects the different rooms and inner courtyards, not only hinting at the spatial experience of traditional Chinese gardens, but also echoing Le Corbusier's promenade architecture. The inspiration for Tsingpu Yangzhou Retreat stems from a typical northern Chinese type of courtyard known as *siheyuan*. Through a grid-like floor plan, Neri&Hu created an inward-facing multi-courtyard space. And just like a *siheyuan*, where visitors pass through a row of courtyards to proceed deeper into the building, the courtyards in Tsingpu Yangzhou Retreat add layers to the spatial experience, while landscape and architecture are blended together by the framing of scenery.

Architects also chose to interpret more unusual architectural types based on the context of the site. Jishou Art Museum by Atelier FCJZ is a perfect combination of a traditional covered bridge and a contemporary art museum. As an ancient type of infrastructure, covered bridges not only meet the obvious functional requirements of crossing rivers and valleys, but also serve as public spaces for people to rest and vendors to set up stalls. Relying on a modern formal language, Jishou Art Museum takes the form of a bridge on top of a bridge, creating a museum that also doubles as a pedestrian overpass. New Campus of Yan'an University by Tsinghua University's Architectural Design & Research Institute is rooted in the unique environment and architectural culture of the region. The ground floor of the new library building borrows spatial characteristics from traditional local cave dwellings to form an open public space, while the upper part of the building is inspired by the setbacks in such cave dwellings, continuing this architectural symbol in an abstract way. AZL Architects reexamined and recreated an old spatial type from a contemporary perspective for BingDing Wood Kiln in Jingdezhen. As a production space, kiln houses were typically supported only by a wooden bent. However, with the imminent disappearance of traditional handicrafts over time, kilns have taken on a symbolic cultural significance today. Therefore, by employing the arch as an ancient form element, AZL Architects has not only continued the structural language of the kiln, but also strengthened the sense of ritual and commemoration in the space.

It is difficult to define gardens as a building type in the strictest sense, but they have indeed influenced the creations of many contemporary Chinese architects in spatial and cultural contexts. Architect Ge Ming, a scholar of classical Chinese gardens, created Spring Garden in the countryside near Taihu Lake in Yixing. It takes the form of a "half garden-half house." Just as classical Chinese gardens resemble real nature, despite being man-made, Spring Garden explores the articulation between nature and man-made creations. The blank spaces between the overlapping roof panels, the reflections on the water, and the transitional shadows and gaps altogether create a latent sense of vitality. Studio Qi's Annso Hill Hotel explores the relationship between the body and space of classical Chinese gardens in a more subtle way. Located in Tengchong, a town on the border of the southern Chinese province of Yunnan, the hotel has a façade that gradually retracts up a 15-meter-high slope. Beneath the recumbent gray-tile roofs, a pure white space rises in sync with the terrain, connecting different public functions, and forming a dialogue with the mountain and the forests through windows and openings of different heights.

Traditional materials and their innovation

The issue of construction technology and type is closely connected to the use and innovation of traditional materials by architects. Traditional construction materials are often linked to local construction techniques, making the application of traditional materials a process of research and experimentation. Yet the innovative combination of traditional materials, modern forms, and contemporary construction techniques frequently leads to the unexpected dialogue between tradition and progress.

For Terra Retreat Boutique Hotel in Dawan Village, on the banks of the Yellow River, Duoxiang Studio utilised a special cement mortar technique to recreate the texture of local rammed earth walls, thereby creating a weathered, aged feel. The reed-covered walkways made of local materials form an ambiguous boundary between the inside and outside of the residential complex of bungalows, terraces, and courtyards. Located in the low-tech environment of the countryside, BingDing Wood Kiln is built with fair-faced concrete, which is well-adapted to local conditions, while hand-fired kiln bricks are used as lattice components for the high window openings. Native yellow sandstone used for the New Campus of Yan'an University library building is based on experiments with yellow sandstone of different hues and manual chiseling directions. The building ultimately presents itself with a heavy yet simple material texture similar to the traditional local cave dwellings.

Light of Internet Conference Center in Wuzhen, designed by Fab-Union Architectural Technology and Digital Fabrication for the World Internet Conference, has a large column-free exhibition hall (90 meters by 200 meters) formed by a roof-ridge string beam structure combined with catenary beams. The conference center also includes four smaller exhibition halls. Just as the World Internet Conference introduced completely different content to this picturesque historic water town, Fab-Union's design also achieved an innovative interpretation of traditional materials through parameterized form-finding techniques, semi-prefabricated parts, and experimental automated construction techniques.

Collective memory and late tradition

If the aforementioned works have formed a connection with the general understanding of traditional Chinese architecture based on construction, type, and materials, does that mean that tradition itself is limited to these categories? When timber structures, white walls, gray tiles, and classical gardens become stereotyped characteristics of traditional Chinese buildings, some architects turn their attention towards places and memories closer to the present.

One historic type of construction that requires preservation and discussion comes from the collective memory of the founding of the People's Republic of China. Qinyong Village, located in Ningbo, was the first village in Zhejiang Province to be designed according to an overarching plan. The scenery of the neat and uniform layout under the commune system differs completely from traditional villages in a patriarchal society. Public buildings such as the primary school, canteen, local guest house, and auditorium form an integral part of the collective memory of the village. Atelier XÜK transformed the former school into a bed-and-breakfast to develop rural tourism, while taking into account the local restraints towards construction costs, scale, and collective memory. Atelier Archmixing's Cotton Lab Urban Lounge in Changzhou, Jiangsu Province, was an ordinary three-span factory. By building a "house-in-house" design, the architects transformed this run-of-the-mill industrial building into an offline experience store integrating new retail concepts for the internet era.

The Tai Kwun Center for Heritage and Arts in Hong Kong is the former home of the city's central police station, magistracy, and prison. The historic building complex is surrounded by walls; its enclosure symbolizing the majesty of the law. Herzog & de Meuron's renovation of the complex redefines this once closed-off space and its inner courtyards as a cultural center for gatherings and communication, while the cast-aluminum exterior units of the façade further echo the existing elements of the site in scale and proportion.

Western tradition in a Chinese context

The acceleration of globalization since the 1990s has made the interpenetration, connection, and influence between countries, regions, and cultures more universal and complex. When discussing the dichotomies of East-West and tradition-modernity against this background, a connection that should not be ignored is how overseas architects bring their own cultural traditions into their Chinese practice, and how the influence of other cultural traditions consciously or unconsciously emerges in the practice of Chinese architects who have studied or worked overseas.

In the design of New Bund District Church, located in Shanghai's New Bund Urban Development Zone, the Spanish architecture firm Ábalos + Sentkiewicz reinterpreted this typical Western building type with modern formal language in the urban Chinese context. The design is closely related to the surrounding public space. The spiraling walkway outside the building leads visitors to the church roof overlooking the surrounding park and Huangpu River, which is reminiscent of the European tradition of cathedral roofs acting as a public platform for the city. The design of the church is also inspired by Ábalos + Sentkiewicz's unbuilt project La Casa Verde (1997), which provided the reference point for the landscape approach to form a connection between the organic shape of the building and the city.

Drawing Architecture Studio is well known for its architectural paintings, and the two-dimensional scenic design strategy is still visible in its spatial practice. In Free Balcony An, the studio playfully collages a number of classical Western elements into one apartment, including an arched window niche, wide storage spaces acting as partitions, and wainscot paneling with light-colored wooden edges. The rich materiality, composed of solid oak, lacquered wood boards, wood veneer, marble, bronze, figured glass, mosaic, and diatomaceous earth, is reminiscent of the interior designs by Adolf Loos.

Tradition and its connection to the present have always been important issues in the development of Chinese architectural practice. From Western academic architects such as Henry Murphy at the beginning of the twentieth century, to the adaptive Chinese architecture that integrated the formal characteristics of classical Chinese buildings, and on to the inherent Chinese style advocated by Liang Sicheng, Lin Huiyin, and the Society for the Study of Chinese Architecture. And from the great discussion of socialist content and a national style in the 1950s, to the recognition of tradition based on semiotics and linguistics under the influence of the postmodernist architectural trend in the 1980s. This edition of *Architecture China* does not intend to provide an ultimate answer to the question of tradition, but rather strives to present insights and possibilities through the practice of 16 architects.

CONTEMPORARY TRANSLATIONS OF TRADITIONAL MATERIALS IN RURAL CONSTRUCTION

Song Wei and Tian Weijia
College of Architecture and Urban Planning, Tongji University

In 2006, as part of the Chinese National Pavilion at the 10th International Architecture Exhibition at the Venice Biennale, Wang Shu designed a courtyard installation called "Tiled Garden." The architect collected tens of thousands of local Chinese tiles and used them to create a roof-like slope in an outdoor garden. He added a lightweight bamboo footbridge above the tiles, allowing visitors to experience walking on the roof of a traditional Chinese building. Wang's installation not only restored the shape and materials of a traditional Chinese roof, but also recreated a vivid spatial experience of traditional Chinese urban life. It is undoubtedly an excellent example of the contemporary translation of China's traditional architectural language.

Ten years later, at the 15th Venice Architecture Biennale in 2016, Wang's Amateur Architecture Studio returned to the language of materials, presenting a series of projects, including Ningbo Museum and the Wencun Village Renovation, while launching a comprehensive discussion on contemporary expressions of traditional materials. In these projects, seemingly ordinary rural building materials, such as bamboo formwork used for pouring concrete, recycled broken tiles, gray bricks assembled through different masonry techniques, and adobe walls, are presented in a new way. Wang's square-shaped material samples displayed at the Venice Biennale represented the challenge that many Chinese architects practicing in the countryside are concerned with: How can these materials be utilized to express the dialogue between the past and present?

future science town and attracting investment, Guangming District is facing unprecedented opportunities to gather wisdom and to integrate outcomes of technology into everyday urban life. The exhibition serves as a progressive image of these pioneering ideas.

Participants shared their research subjects and exhibition ideas in the forum. The keynote speech by Professor Michael Speaks, dean of the School of Architecture at Syracuse University, launched a reflective criticism of big data as a tool of urban planning. He warned urban planners about the risk of losing the initiative completely to computer calculation. In response, data scientist Dr. Cai Ronghua and his team from Singapore shared with the audience their latest application of urban data in the management system of cities. The debate on the advantages and disadvantages of big data was even extended by some other exhibitors' presentations on relevant topics.

In the roundtable discussion, urban planning, transportation, energy, and telecommunications researchers debated the influences that technology imposes on urban development. Most participants were optimistic that urban development benefits from innovative science and technology. The exhibition venue was located in the Exhibition Center of Guangming Science Town to better showcase the future technology. Curator Yin Yujun explained that it was a typical presentation of the urban nomadic exhibition mode of UABB, and it took only 55 days to finish the Exhibition Center from the preliminary design to final completion. This "Shenzhen speed" exhibited the ambition of Guangming District to embody the idea of embracing science and technology.

After fruitful discussions in the forum, the opening ceremony successfully rang down the curtain. A series of lectures, seminars, and workshops will be organized in the coming three months of the exhibition to bring about the collision of innovative ideas among architects, urban planners, artists, and urban administrators. Interactive performances and immersive activities will also be organized.

All photos © Zhang Chao

that Isozaki's contribution to architecture is not only in his works, but also in his ideas.

Professor Li Xiangning asked Isozaki what he thought, at his current age, of his predecessors and newcomers. Isozaki stated that he had learned much from his predecessors, while also admiring some of the younger architects for doing interesting things he hadn't done—or couldn't do—himself.

Architect Xing Tonghe praised Isozaki for his unlimited creativity, experience, and support for the younger generation of architects. He asked him how he saw the lacking degree of completion of some projects in China. Isozaki said that when he first arrived in China, he discovered that the country was bigger and more sublime than Japan, referring to the concept of "greater number," which he had mentioned earlier in his lecture when talking about "number, greater number, and hyper number."

Architect Zhang Lei once invited Isozaki to visit the architectural works of Nanjing. When visiting Tonglu, they saw the typical southern Chinese landscape, which reminded Isozaki of a certain Japanese school of painting. The two also talked about Lu Yu, China's Sage of Tea. Zhang asserted that Isozaki had a very profound understanding of Chinese culture. Liu Yichun claimed that the remnants of the Tsukuba Center as an architectural concept influenced his work. Isozaki's book *Japan-ness in Architecture* (2003) shows how to understand the notions of Japan-ness from the outside looking in, and how his work in Japan stems from the external observation of this phenomenon. Therefore, Japan-ness exists only outside Japan and not within the country itself.

A master of continuous creativity and imagination, Isozaki's architecture is characterized by idealism, self-denial, and critical tendencies. The Pritzker Prize was a tribute to Isozaki's career in architecture, and his influence on modern architecture will not end there. His path still continues.

Photo © Architectural Design and Research Institute of Tongji University

Opening of the 2019 UABB Sub-venue of Guangming

The opening ceremony of the 8th UABB (Bi-City Biennale of Urbanism\Architecture) sub-venue of Guangming District was held on December 22, 2019. With the theme "Guangming Inter-connected Future," this sub-venue promotes Guangming District as a future pioneer in scientific exploration and urban construction.

After a short film, the main curator, Yin Yujun, introduced the curation direction as well as exhibition highlights. There are multiple meanings in the Chinese term "Guangming" (光明). It is the name of the newly established municipal district in 2018, which used to be famous for its agricultural products. Literally, it means "shining bright," which is to indicate a bright future for the new district. In the "Outline of the Development Plan for the Guangdong-Hong Kong-Macau Greater Bay Area" delivered by the State Council in February 2019, the city of Shenzhen plays a fundamental role, as the planning of a new science town in Guangming District is in response to central government. The shift from agriculture to high-tech culture became the general background for the exhibition. By proposing the idea of inter-connection, the curator strove to present the potentiality of multifold urban spatial strategies in the linkage of human beings to nature, technology, and the internet.

The first sub-venue set up in Guangming District was for the 2017 UABB and themed "Renovation of Jingkou: The Remaking of Garden Community in Urban Context of High Density." The exhibition provided a development path of sustainability for communities by revealing the hidden values of natural resources. This time, by inviting institutes of frontier scientific research into the

Arata Isozaki Retrospective Lecture Series: Contemporary Architect

On December 11, 2019, internationally renowned architect and 2019 Pritzker Prize winner Arata Isozaki gave an academic lecture at the Architectural Design and Research Institute of Tongji University, and was awarded the title of honorary professor by the university.

This was Isozaki's fifth retrospective lecture on the Japanese space-time concept of "*ma*." The theme of the lecture, "Contemporary Architect," further explored Isozaki's concept of "number" on the basis of *ma*, providing the audience with cultural ideas far beyond architecture itself.

Isozaki's academic report began with introducing *ma*. While the words time and space are considered two sides of the same coin in European culture, the Chinese characters 時 (time, hour) and 空 (space, emptiness) first appeared about 150 years ago and are both combined with the character 間 (*ma*) to form concepts and dimensions of space and time. In 1987, when Isozaki gave a lecture at Tongji University, he had already started to introduce the concept of *ma*. As a native Japanese architect and cultural intermediary between Asia and Europe, he has since been constantly asked by Western audiences why his designs seemingly look Western, but are ultimately different. Where do these different thoughts and outputs on space and time originate from?

Apart from *ma*, Isozaki also explored the character 霊 (spirit) in his lecture. The Japanese concept of time was known as 時霊 (zeitgeist), but beginning in the late 1980s it was used less and less. Instead the combination of 霊 with the character 地 (earth) appeared, meaning "genius loci" when combined. Specific Asian concepts were used to study corresponding problems of space in architectural design or in the military. However, English and Chinese translations of these two words create some issues of differentiation. As for how to think about the meaning of these words, Isozaki found a common thread: "number."

The concept of architecture is full of differences between Eastern and Western contexts. Such discrepancies and dislocations often result in the discussion and emergence of new concepts. The English term "architecture" used to be known as "techniques of construction" in ancient China, while in Japan it was described as "rules" and "construction twine," further showing how it has a wide range of meanings in different cultures.

Starting with the term "architect" itself, architects have stemmed into three distinct identities: artists, engineers, and strategists, with different meanings and working states in different contexts. When thinking about architecture from the perspective of the design and engineering processes, Frank Lloyd Wright is a typical "artist architect," while Norman Foster is representative of the "engineer architect." In many current English publications, the term "architect" is also used to describe those who plan and strategize, not just people who design buildings.

After the academic report, Isozaki and the audience discussed the topic of "contemporary architects." Several guests recalled their time as students, copying Isozaki's newly built Tsukuba Center Building, which they said had influenced an entire generation of Chinese architects.

Professor Zhi Wenjun reviewed the comments and reports of Chinese architectural media on Arata Isozaki. In the second issue of *Time + Architecture* in 1988, Isozaki was introduced academically for the first time. Zhi believes

Zhuang Weimin and Meinhard von Gerkan win the 2019 Liang Sicheng Architecture Prize

The Liang Sicheng Architecture Prize was awarded to Zhuang Weimin and Meinhard von Gerkan at an award ceremony on September 24, 2019, held at the China Hall of Science and Technology in Beijing. The Ministry of Construction of the People's Republic of China and the Architectural Society of China established the award in 2000. Since 2016, it has been awarded internationally and is the highest honor awarded to architects in China. Zhuang Weimin is currently the dean, professor, and doctoral supervisor of the School of Architecture at Tsinghua University, as well as dean and chief architect of the Architectural Design & Research Institute of Tsinghua University. He has presided over the architectural design work for major projects such as the renovation of the National Art Museum of China, the 2008 Summer Olympics Beijing Shooting Range Hall, and the National Exhibition and Convention Center (Shanghai).

Meinhard von Gerkan is a German architect and founding partner of gmp Architects (von Gerkan, Marg and Partners). His architectural design projects include the Berlin-Tegel Airport, renovation and expansion of the National Museum of China, and planning of Qingdao Grand Theatre and Shanghai's Lingang New City.

"Building a Future Countryside" Touring Exhibition at the Curitiba Biennial in Brazil

Supported by the China National Arts Fund, the second leg of the international "Building a Future Countryside" exhibition tour kicked off on September 21, 2019, at the 14th Curitiba International Biennial of Contemporary Art at Museu Oscar Niemeyer in Curitiba, Brazil. One of the most influential biennales in Latin America, the Curitiba Biennial was themed "Open Border." Curator Tereza de Arruda believes the Chinese rural experience presented in "Building a Future Countryside" demonstrates the experience of opening cultural boundaries.

Tongji University organized and implemented "Building a Future Countryside," and it builds on the exhibition content of the Pavilion of China at the 16th Venice Architecture Biennale in 2018. The practical experience of Chinese architectural art is fully showcased by the architectural models, drawings, photographs, and videos in the exhibition.

According to Li Xiangning, chief curator of "Building a Future Countryside" and professor at Tongji University's College of Architecture and Urban Planning, one of the major challenges facing the built environment is the future development of the countryside. But a new generation of architects, planners, and artists are going beyond creating exceptional individual projects in the rural environment. They are trying to extend such projects into a series of multi-angle, multilevel construction acts and social activities to continuously participate in the transformation of the rural environment, the development of the rural economy, the extension of the farmer's way of life, and even a cultural renaissance. Through a panoramic view of the Chinese countryside, as well as the presentation of projects for rural housing, local industry, traditional practices, agricultural tourism, and community revitalization, the exhibition shows the incorporation of Chinese architectural practices in the construction of rural work and cultural pursuits. It outlines the new prospects of the contemporary rural Chinese countryside and explores a new model for future rural development.

All photos © Gao Changjun

1. Tiled Garden © Chen Lichao
2. Ningbo Museum © Chen Lichao

Bamboo, wood, tiles, bricks, stone, and earth carry the label of being traditional and have frequently appeared in rural construction across China in recent years. In contemporary practice, a new generation of architects has been trying to breach traditional methods of construction through the extended study and application of traditional materials and techniques, thus conforming with the zeitgeist. However, the breakthroughs and innovation of materials and techniques will inevitably run into the expressionist mistake, which is contrary to the authentic nature of the materials. Presently, contemporary Chinese architects are still meandering and debating over the intersection between tradition and the contemporary.

Bamboo

Bamboo is an important carrier of Chinese culture. Along with the plum tree, orchid, and chrysanthemum, bamboo has been regarded as a plant that is representative of the ideal character traits of a gentleman scholar. Bamboo signifies perseverance, openheartedness, and uprightness. These connotations originate from the plant's unique biological properties, such as its nodes and hollow structure, which are also the same characters used in the Chinese word for "moral integrity" (竹) . The famous Song dynasty poet Su Shi once wrote of bamboo: "Having no meat to eat is better than not having bamboo in one's life. Not eating meat makes people thin, but not having bamboo makes people vulgar. Thin people can still become fat, but there's no cure for vulgarity."

Having become an important part of traditional Chinese landscapes, the fondness of bamboo continues to this day. For architects, in addition to the cultural implications, the physical characteristics of bamboo and its inherent mechanical resistance to torsion also provide broad opportunities for its usage. Beijing architect Xu Tiantian designed Bamboo Theatre with still-growing bamboo in Hengkeng Village, Songyang County, in Eastern China's Zhejiang Province. Local operas are performed on the stage during holidays, and villagers use the space to rest and chat after a day of working in the mountains on ordinary days.

The architect wove bamboo stems into a dome as they were growing, making full use of the plant's rapid growth and flexibility. He thus combined a dome—a classical Western architectural element—with a traditional

Bamboo Theater © Wang Ziling

technique used in bamboo-lined walkways, while visually expressing a rural low-tech construction context and eco-friendly building concepts. Once the bamboo around the central stage of the theater was woven and fixed into place, the growing parts at the end of the branches required little maintenance, and new branches and leaves could fill in the existing grid. This organic architectural language has thus gained stability and immortality in its original natural environment.

The use of living plants as a building material is the most unique design idea found in this project. Seasonal restrictions and time constraints inspired the architect to weave the bamboo during the slow growth period of autumn and winter, and to take advantage of the rapid growth experienced during spring. In doing so, Xu created a public space that fully demonstrates the innovative strategies that result from the material limitations in rural construction.

In addition to the flexibility of bamboo, the dense vertical texture of bamboo forests has also influenced the practice of contemporary architects. Wang Shu used bamboo formwork to cast concrete walls with bamboo texture at Fuchun Cultural Complex in Hangzhou's Fuyang District. This strategy was inspired by the ocean-like bamboo forests near Fuyang. The technique creates a unique interplay between the building and the environment as the bamboo-textured interior walls present visitors with the illusion of passing through an outdoor bamboo forest. Although the use of bamboo to make concrete molds is relatively rare, it resembles a northern European regional practice, establishing a connection to the local context through raw molds. Compared to Xu Tiantian's Bamboo Theatre, it still has a certain degree of reproducibility. A similar use of bamboo can also be found at Sifang Art Museum, designed by American architect Steven Holl, in Nanjing.

Bamboo formwork gives texture to concrete at Fuchun Cultural Complex © Lv Hengzhong

Stone Nest Amphitheatre © Jin Weiqi

Stone

Hakka Indenture Museum—another project by Xu Tiantian, in Songyang County—clearly shows the charm of traditional stonework, with the building walls entirely made of rubble. Even though only one material is used, different masonry techniques are employed for a more sensible construction logic at the building's transitions and openings. The architect used large quoins for each outside corner to provide better static support and visually emphasize the rigidity and strength of the turns. Angled stones sit ceremoniously on top of the door jambs to hold up the lintel—another traditional masonry technique. Unified perpend stones are used in large quantities to hold together the stones of the nearly 1-meter-thick walls. A small artificial canal inside the building was originally used for drainage in the village. The canal was not only kept after the new building was completed, but the architect also constructed an overhead skylight that mimics its shape. The skylight is uncovered, so that rainwater drips through the opening and into the drainage canal. A water curtain will form during heavy rain, and a rainbow may emerge in the sunlight.

Hakka Indenture Museum © Wang Ziling

Architect He Wei used stone masonry for Stone Nest Amphitheatre in Weihai, Shandong Province, to form a dialogue between the amphitheater and the quarry behind it. The irregular, broken lines of the stone platforms, and the quarried backdrop, surround and create the central stage, entering into an intertextual relationship with the environment. A café is also incorporated beneath the elevated stage and seating. Most of the stones are from the site when it was leveled, with the variety of treatment methods of the same material depicting different human attitudes toward the rural landscape in different phases.

The Macha Village Center © Wu Zhi Qiao Charitable Foundation

Rammed earth

Rammed earth is the oldest and most widely used construction technique in China. A nationwide census organized by the Ministry of Housing and Urban-Rural Development between 2010 and 2011 revealed there are still at least 60 million people across China living in different types of buildings made of earth. These include the more widely known traditional cave dwellings of the Yellow River Loess Plateau and the *tulou* earthen buildings of southern China's Fujian Province, as well as *mogufang* (or mushroom houses), Tuzhangfang in Southwest China, the earthen towers on the Qinghai-Tibet Plateau, and the mud-brick houses of the ancient city of Kashgar in Xinjiang.

Architect Mu Jun, professor at Beijing University of Civil Engineering and Architecture, studied the design and construction of rammed earth architecture for more than 10 years. He described the modern improved rammed earth buildings as the most direct bridge connecting tradition and modernity. Buildings made of earth not only have a natural advantage in terms of thermal performance, but after the improvement on their weaknesses such as earthquake resistance and compactness through modern technology, their application in the countryside provides even more unique opportunities.

Architect Mu Jun combined improved rammed earth techniques with green building technology for Macha Village Center. A single-pitched roof on the three-sided building facilitates rainwater collection in the center of the courtyard, and small wind turbines provide half of the building's electricity. Its rammed earth walls were constructed traditionally without the help of professional builders. Characteristics such as minimal operating costs, ease of construction, and high fault tolerance allow for a wide applicability of this low-threshold rural approach.

Due to the natural simplicity of this material, rammed earth can also be misused in projects. Simulating rammed earth by simply coating the building with the material also points towards the phenomenon of "superficial contextualization" in Chinese rural construction.

Tiles

The façade wall of Ningbo Museum, designed by Wang Shu, provides a direct dialogue between the past and present, with a local architectural craft known as "*wapan* wall," which is made of stacked tiles. However, a *wapan* wall is not a simple pile of materials, but rather an exquisite craft of construction. First, it is necessary to use intact stones for the base of the wall. Then, all kinds of broken bricks and tiles are stacked to create the upper layers, with the fragments leveled out to ensure there are no excess gaps in the wall. A thin layer of lime is applied for reinforcement and to complete the *wapan* wall. The wall has been gradually forgotten with the advent of modern mass production as its construction process relies on refined manual operation.

To apply this technique on the outer wall of Ningbo Museum, the builders collected a large number of old bricks and tiles, including gray bricks, hollow bricks, tiles, and ceramic pot pieces, many of which stem from the Ming and Qing dynasties. This variety forms abstract patterns and textures across the wall, becoming

Recycled tiles on the exterior walls of Ningbo Museum © Chen Lichao

a classic example of the contemporary translation of traditional crafts. Wang Shu applied the same technique to the outer wall of Ningbo Tengtou Pavilion at the Expo 2010 Shanghai China world exposition. The outside wall is made with 600,000 old tiles and bricks collected from nearby towns, such as Fenghua and Yinzhou.

Compared to the manual arrangement of the *wapan* walls of Ningbo Museum and Ningbo Tengtou Pavilion, In Bamboo, designed by Philip F. Yuan and built in the outskirts of Chengdu in Sichuan Province, was completely digitized, optimizing the classic construction model of a wooden structure with tiled roof. Based on a prefabricated wood-and-steel structure, and with the help of a mechanical arm, the infinity-shaped design of the cultural center combines the temperament of traditional architecture with the finesse of contemporary industrial production. The partial separation between construction and site redefines the concept of localization, which is common in China's rural construction, and opens up the possibility of applying new technology in rural areas.

As an old Chinese proverb states: "Seeing an object, and being reminded." Chinese people's love of traditional materials is not a simple obsession, but a way of using bamboo, wood, tiles, bricks, stone, and earth to establish a connection to the past within the present time and space. A clear continuity is all the more important in rural China as it has not yet been hit by a large influx of capital. The efforts of architects to explore new ways of using traditional materials can be seen as a struggle against the irreversible trend of capital and the spread of technology into the countryside, while extending the lifespan of traditional workmanship in our time.

JISHOU ART MUSEUM

Atelier FCJZ

Location: Qianzhou, Jishou, Hunan Province
Architect: Atelier FCJZ
Principal architects: Yung Ho Chang, Lu Lijia
Design team: Liang Xiaoning, Yang Pu, Liu Kunpeng, Su Siqi, Rao Gang
Structural consultant and design: Chang Qiang
Collaboration: Hunan Provincial Communications Planning, Survey & Design Institute co., Ltd.
Area: 3,535 square meters
Design period: 2013–2016
Project completion: 2019
Photography: Tian Fangfang

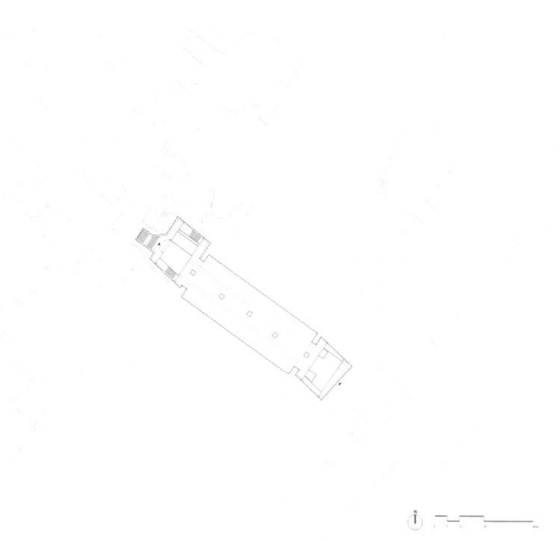

Site plan

Jishou Art Museum is located in Jishou, the capital of the Xiangxi Tujia and Miao Autonomous Prefecture in the west of Hunan Province. The municipal government initially considered a development zone for the museum outside of the city, and indeed nowadays many contemporary cultural facilities are treated as independent monuments and placed far away from their corresponding communities. However, Atelier FCJZ believed the art museum should not be geographically separated from its intended audience. The architects believed it should be implanted into the existing urban fabric, and proposed the museum be located in the center of the densely populated Qianzhou old town district, where residents could easily access it.

Jishou Art Museum is implanted within the existing urban fabric

Jishou Art Museum spans Wanrong River

Atelier FCJZ conceived the art museum to span Wanrong River, which flows through the central area of the city, and it doubles as a walking bridge. They wanted residents to not only make dedicated trips to see the museum, but also to encounter it on their way to work, school, and other daily activities.

Sheltered bridges, known as "wind and rain bridges," have a long history in the mountainous areas of China. In addition to functioning as river or valley crossings, they serve as public spaces for travelers to rest and for vendors to set up stalls. Atelier FCJZ's design is a contemporary interpretation of this ancient form of architecture, introducing new artistic content and modernizing its formal language while maintaining the traditional function.

The entrances to Jishou Art Museum are located on both sides of Wanrong River

Entrance on west side of Wanrong River

Exterior of the main exhibition hall

Entrance on east side of Wanrong River

Pedestrian bridge looking into the main exhibition hall

Pedestrian bridge

East entry lobby

East lobby staircase

Main exhibition hall

1 1. View from the third-floor balcony

2 2. Upper gallery inside the concrete bridge

3 3. Main exhibition hall under the concrete bridge

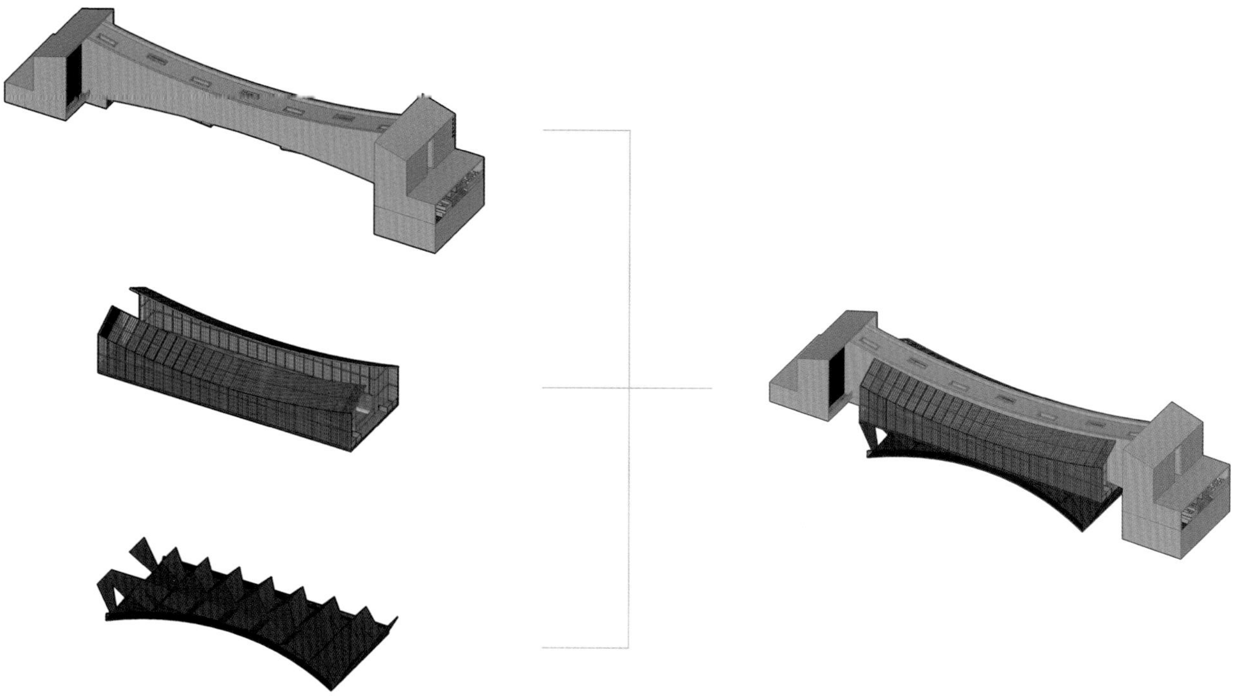

Structural composition

Traditional "wind and rain bridges" © Atelier FCJZ

1 | 2
3 | 4

1. Close up of steel bridge structure
2. Riverside façade with tiled shading
3. Transitional space with post-tensioned prestressing bolt for the concrete bridge
4. A glass wall and tubular-tile shading system encloses the large exhibition hall

The building is composed of two levels layered on top of one another. The lower level is an open steel truss structure that provides a covered walkway for pedestrians and allows the flow of floods beneath it. The upper level is a cast-in-situ concrete arch with a painting gallery inside. Between the two levels, a glass wall and a shading system with tubular tiles encloses a large exhibition hall for temporary exhibitions. The service facilities of the museum, including the foyers, administrative offices, shops, and tearooms, are placed in the buildings at both ends of the bridge.

These buildings are closely connected to the terraced houses on the banks of Wanrong River. The townhouses accommodate shops, restaurants, and small hotels, while the respective homeowners usually occupy the upstairs areas. The entrances to Jishou Art Museum, situated on both sides of the river, blend into the street environment and integrate the museum into the daily life of the local people.

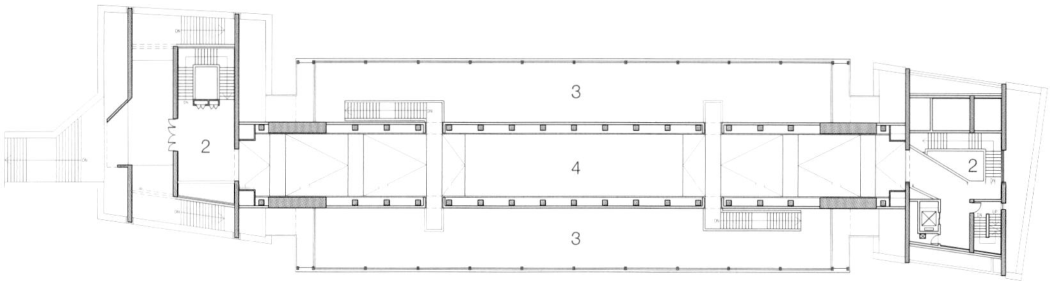

Third-floor plan

2. Lobby
3. Void above main exhibition hall
4. Upper gallery

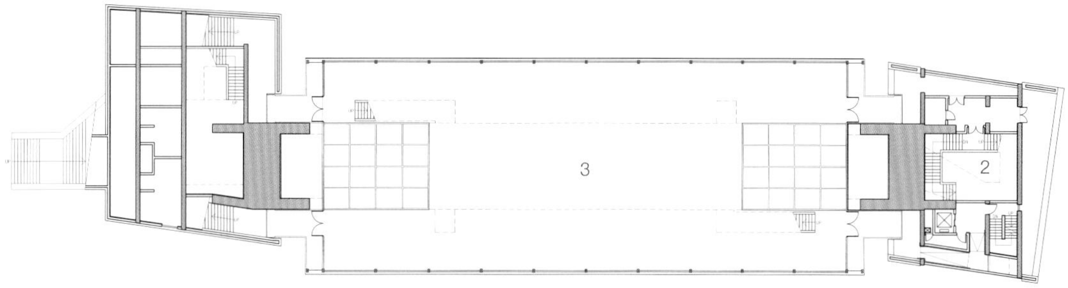

Second-floor plan

2. Void above lobby
3. Main exhibition hall

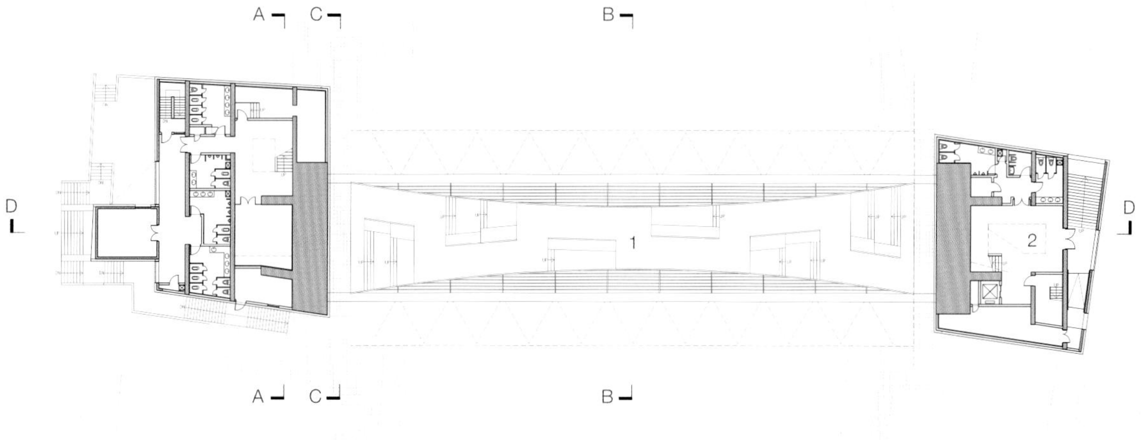

First-floor plan

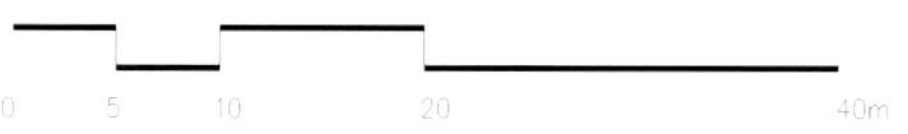

1. Pedestrian bridge
2. Lobby

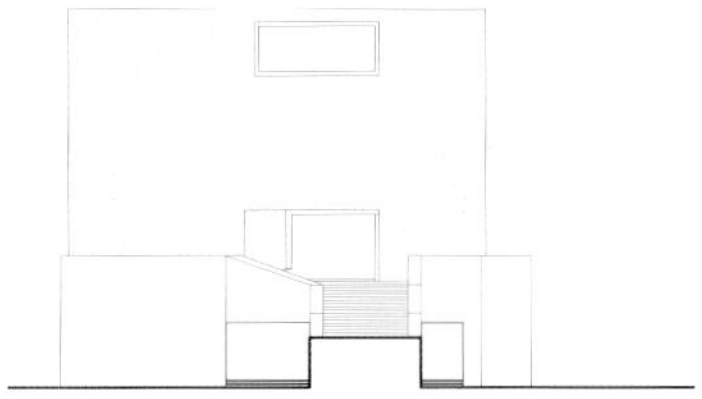

West elevation

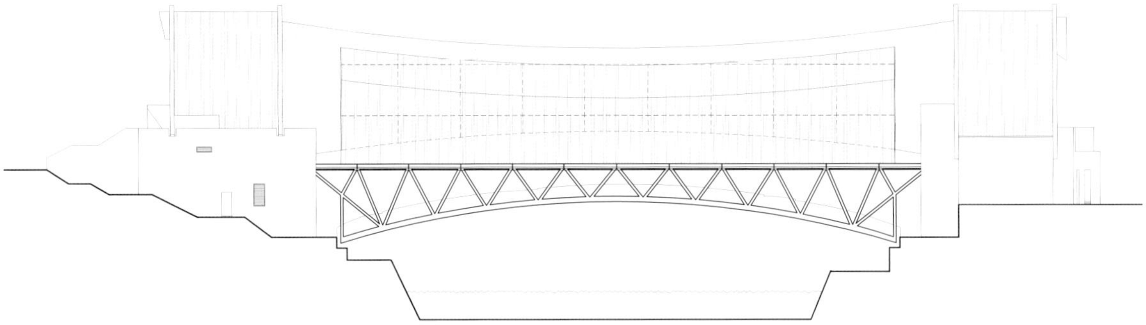

South elevation

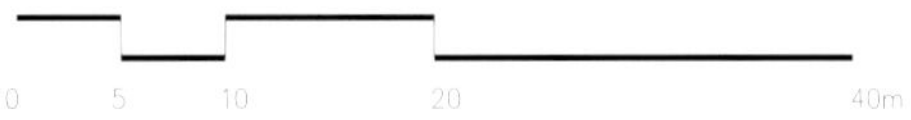

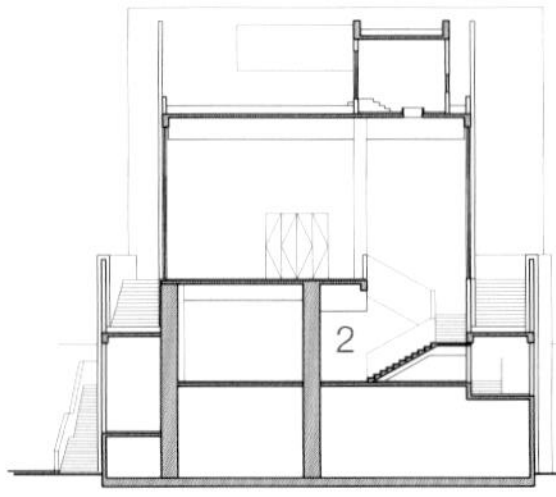

Section A-A

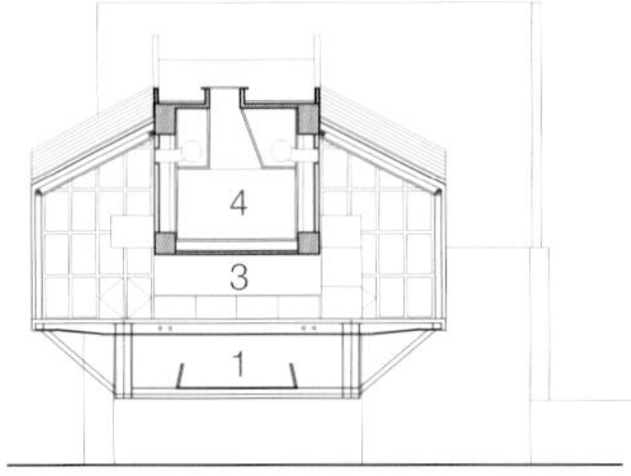

Section B-B

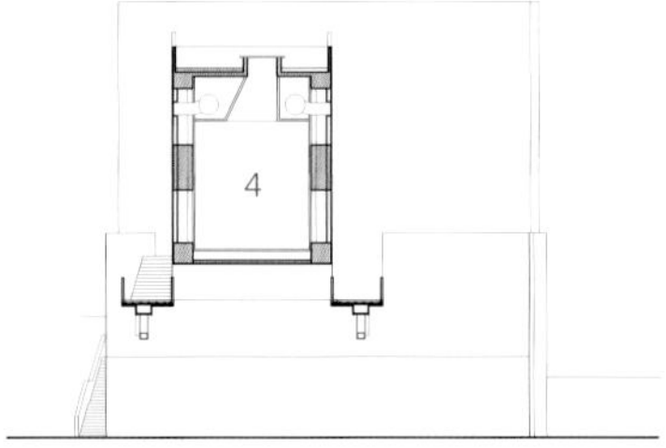

Section C-C

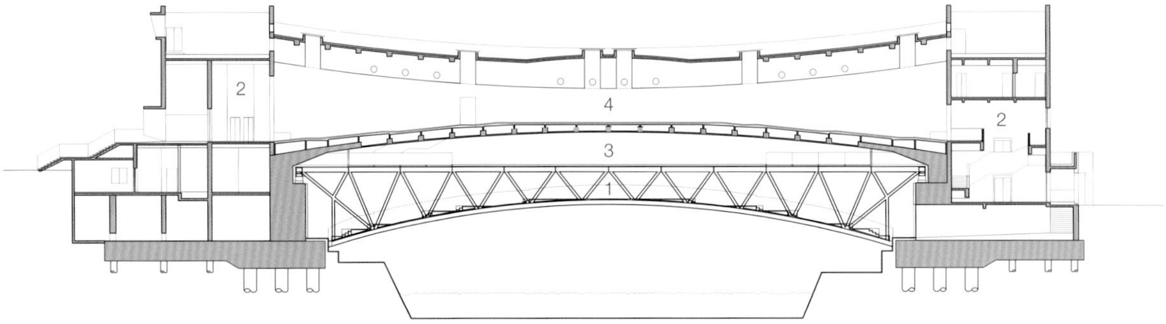

Section D-D

1. Pedestrian bridge
2. Lobby
3. Main exhibition hall
4. Upper gallery

TSINGPU YANGZHOU RETREAT

Neri&Hu Design and Research Office

Location: Hanjiang District, Yangzhou, Jiangsu Province
Architect: Neri&Hu Design and Research Office
Principal architects: Rossana Hu, Lyndon Neri
Design team: Federico Saralvo, Cao Ziyi, Huang Fong, Sela Lim, Zhao Lei, Callum Holgate, Chen Leyue, Valentina Brunetti, Shen Sean, Liu Xin, Zhu Bin, Nicolas Fardet, Wang Yun, Zhang Jin
Area: Site: 32,000 square meters; floor: 4,200 square meters
Design period: 2015–2017
Photography: Pedro Pegenaute

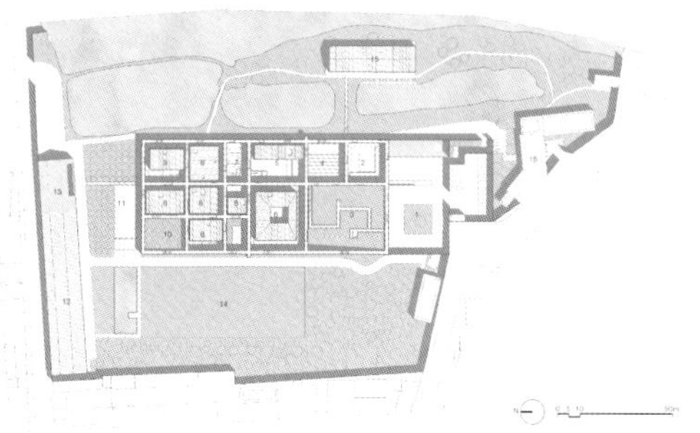

Site plan

Dotted with small lakes and existing structures, the site of Tsingpu Yangzhou Retreat, in close proximity to Yangzhou's scenic Slender West Lake, was a challenging location. The design brief for the 20-room boutique hotel required the adaptive reuse of a series of old buildings that have been renovatd and extended to accommodate the hotel's needs. Neri&Hu unified these scattered elements with a network of gridded walls and paths, tying the project together and enclosing multiple courtyards.

The inspiration for this design originated with the courtyard house typology of vernacular Chinese architecture. As with the traditional courtyard, the courtyards in Tsingpu Yangzhou Retreat give hierarchy to the spaces, frame views of the earth and sky, encapsulate landscape within architecture, and create an overlap between interior and exterior.

Inner courtyard

View of the walled complex from above

Constructed with reclaimed gray brick sourced from the surrounding area, the gridded walls enclose the pathways that provide access to guest rooms and hotel amenities. These narrow interior passageways force a long perspective, and light plays off the various brick patterns, enticing guests to venture deeper into the building. There is a clear separation between the walls and the buildings, with the walls being slightly higher than many of the roof lines so that they are not visible from afar. The walls and buildings also enclose multiple courtyards, some adjoining the guest rooms and shared amenities, such as the reception, library, and restaurant, and others that are unoccupied pockets of garden to offer relief from the sense of enclosure.

View from water pond

Inner courtyard with water pond

Detail of brick wall

Reception area

1 | 2
3
4

1–3. Passageways between the brick walls
4. Sketch of passageway beteween the brick walls

1 / 2

1. Reception and tea room
2. Sunken courtyard between the lakeshore guest rooms

Stairs and openings within the gridded walls provide guests with vantage points to view the building and landscape from above. A multipurpose building, housing a restaurant, theater and exhibition space, is located at the farthest end of the site in a formerly derelict warehouse building. Neri&Hu renovated the existing structure with a concrete addition. Neri&Hu's design for Tsingpu Yangzhou Retreat unifies the complex site and program with a grid of brick walls that also provides a rustic materiality and layering of space that redefines traditional architecture with a modern design language.

View from water pond

Guest rooms

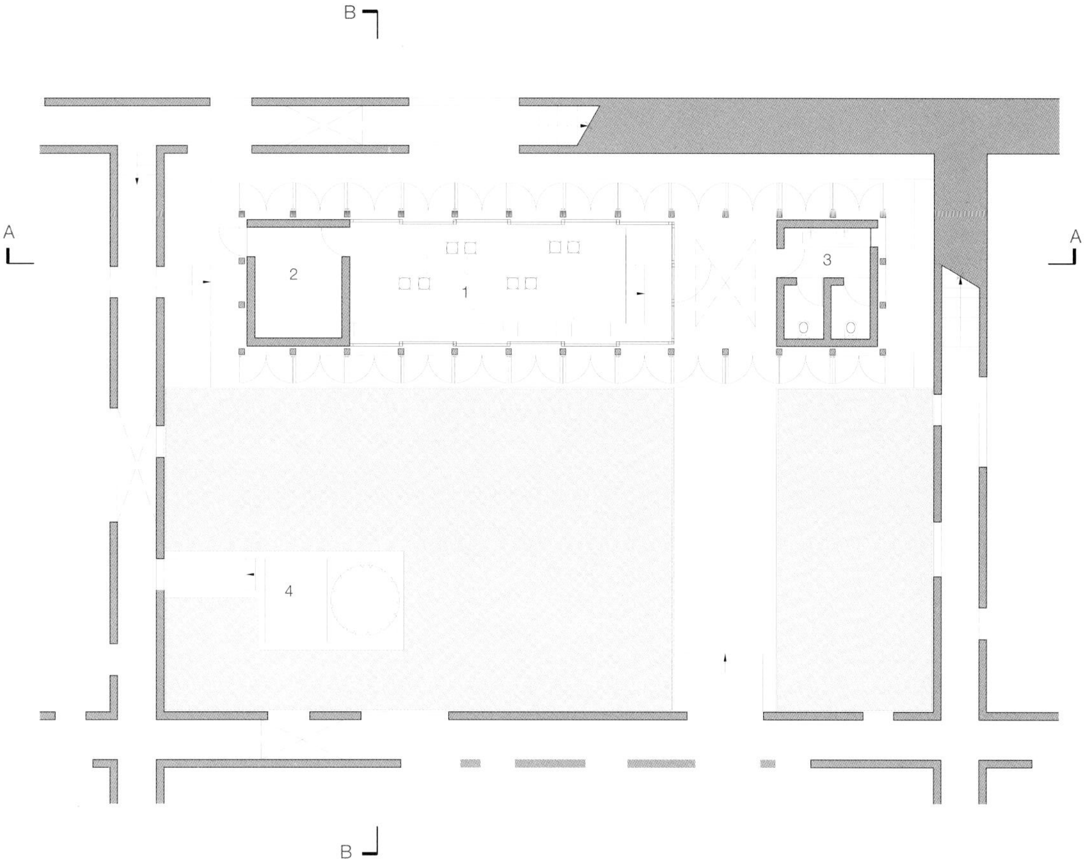

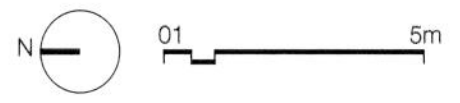

Plan of reception and courtyard

1. Reception and tearoom
2. Office
3. Restrooms
4. Courtyard

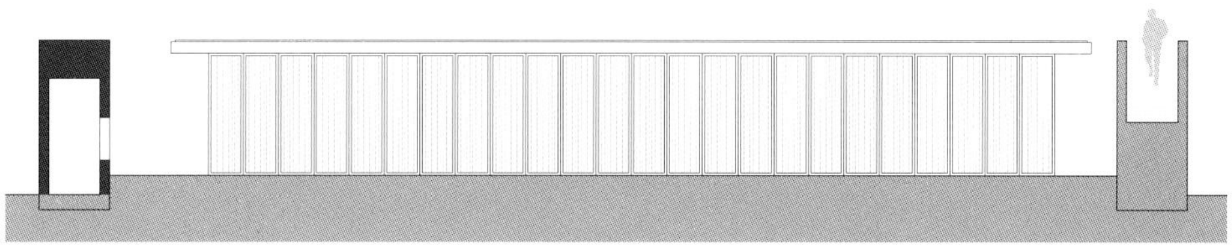

Elevation

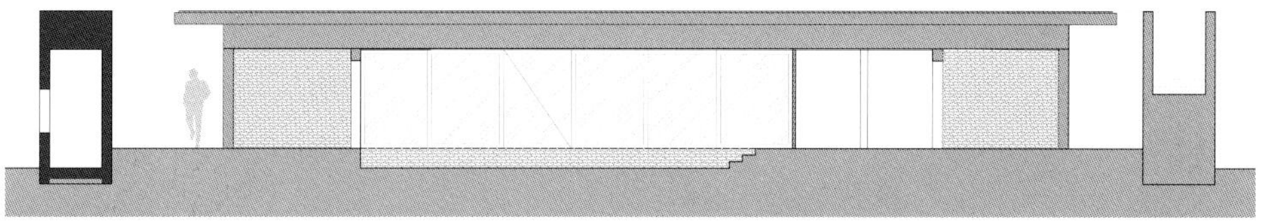

Section A-A

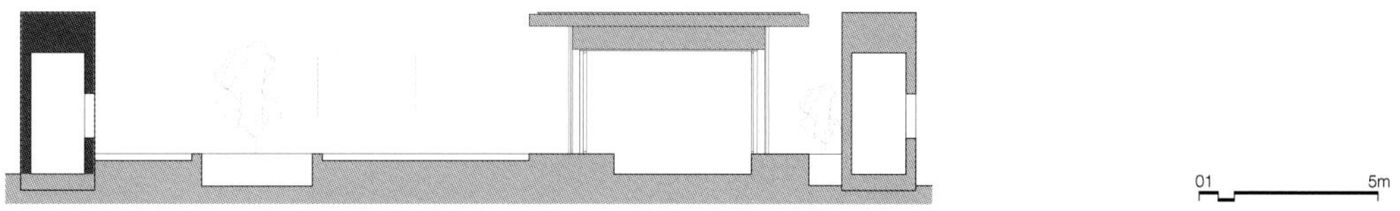

Section B-B

Plan of courtyard guest rooms

1. Outdoor courtyard
2. Guest room
3. Brick-wall passageway

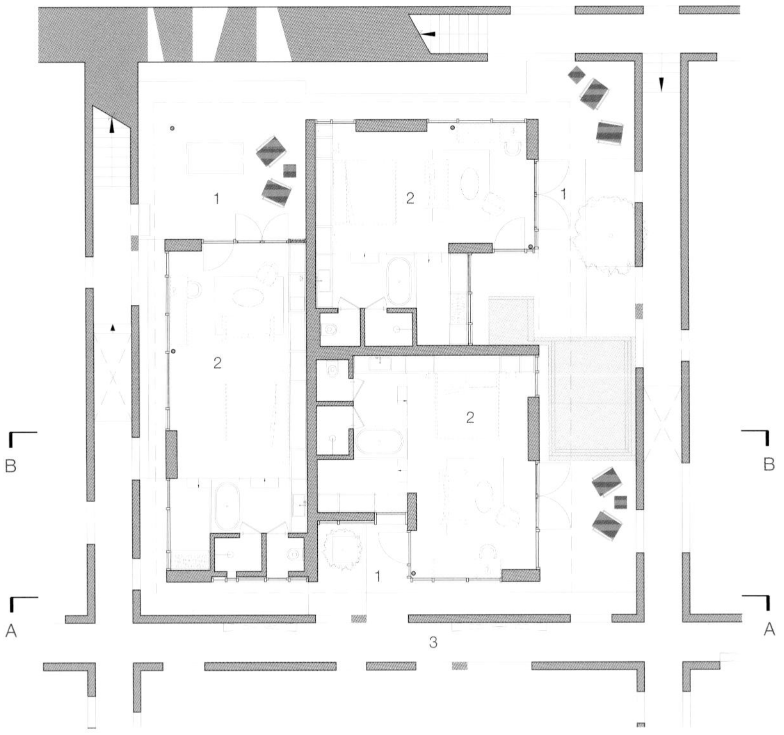

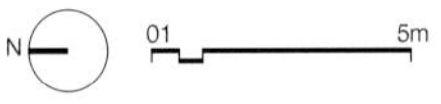

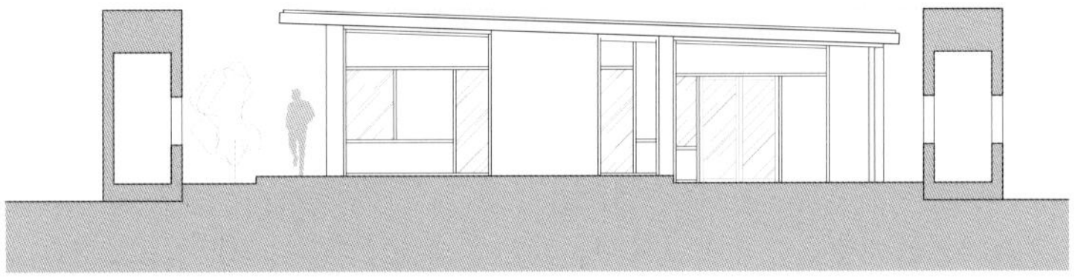

Section A-A

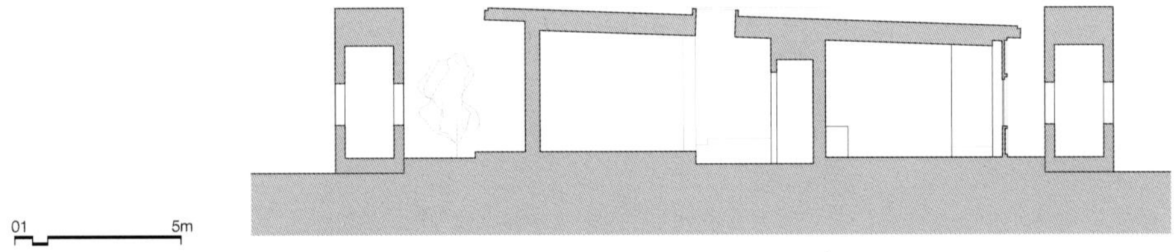

Section B-B

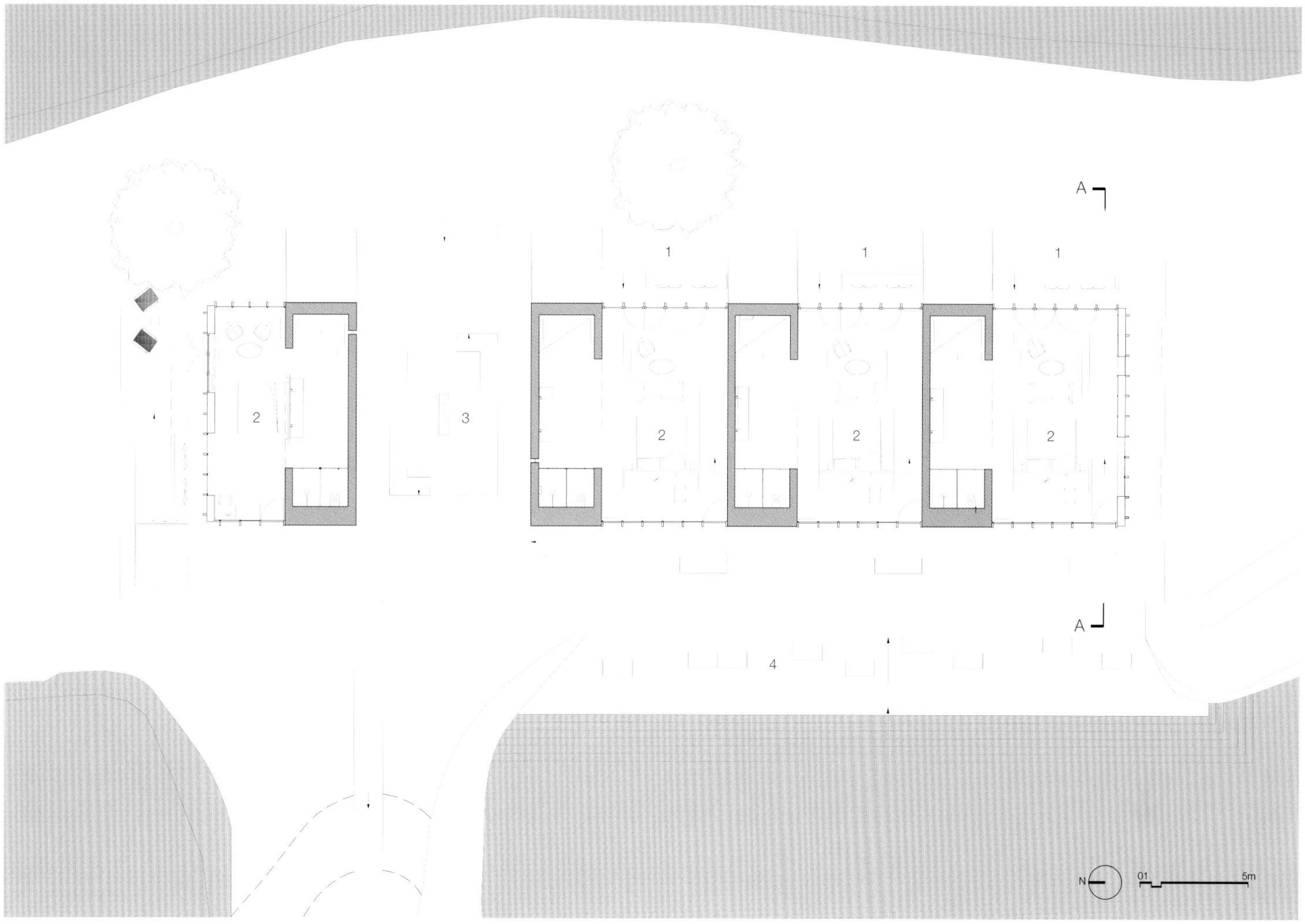

Plan of lakeshore guest rooms

1. Outdoor courtyard
2. Guest room
3. Sunken lounge with fire pit
4. Outdoor seating

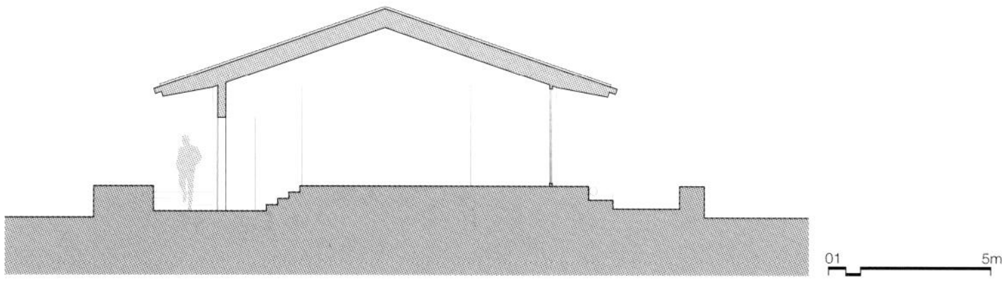

Section A-A

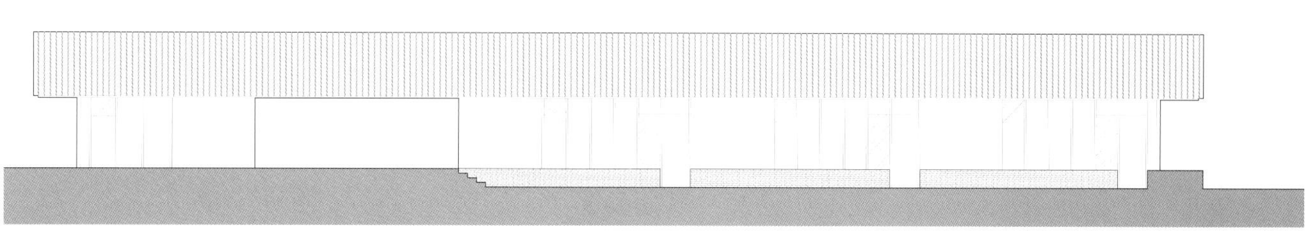

West elevation

Plan of library guest rooms

1. Outdoor courtyard
2. Guest rooms
3. Brick-wall passageway
4. Courtyard
5. Staircase

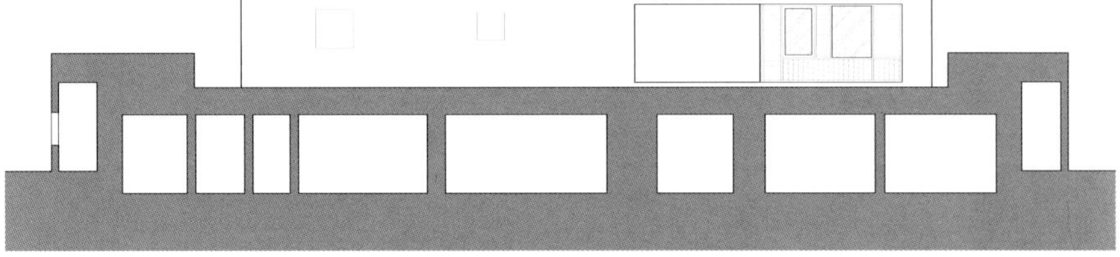
Section A-A

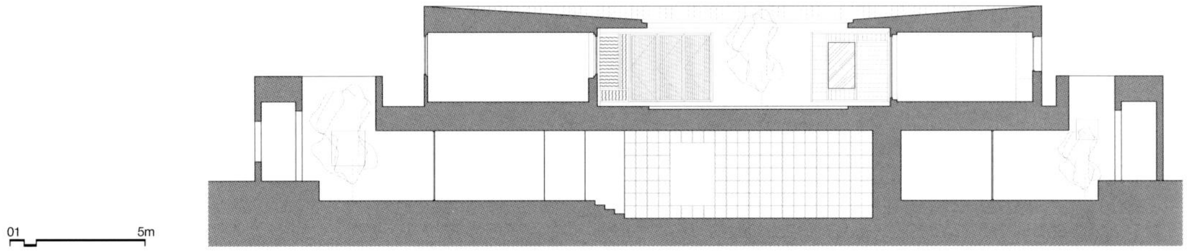

Section B-B

TAI KWUN CENTER FOR HERITAGE AND ART

Herzog & de Meuron

Location: Central, Hong Kong
Architect: Herzog & de Meuron
Principal architects: Jacques Herzog, Pierre de Meuron, Ascan Mergenthaler
Project Team: Edman Choy (associate, project director), Chi-Yan Chan (project manager), Dannes Kok, Vladimir Pajkic (associate, project director), Raymond Jr. Gaëtan (associate)
Executive architect: Rocco Design Architects Associates Ltd.
Conservation architect: Purcell, London, UK
Structural engineer: Arup Hong Kong and Arup London
Area: Site: 14,500 square meters; floor: 27,000 square meters
Project completion: 2018
Photography: Iwan Baan

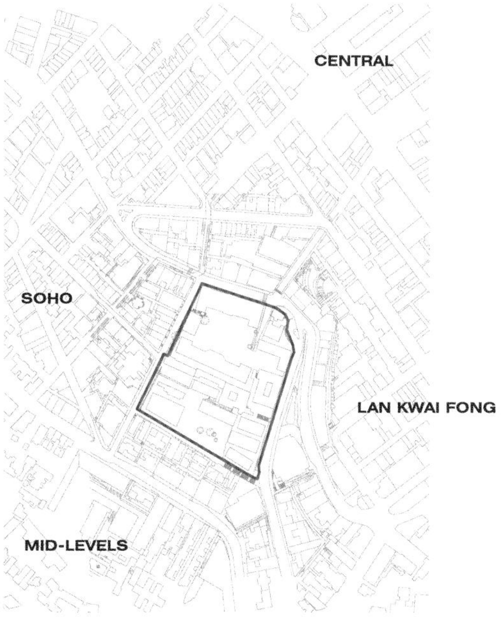

Site plan

The former Central Police Station, Central Magistracy, and Victoria Prison is a walled compound of heritage buildings in the commercial center of Hong Kong Island. Established by the British after 1841 as the colony's main police station, magistracy, and prison, the site is one of Hong Kong's most important remaining historic monuments. The entire compound was vacated following its decommission in 2016, leaving a collection of unique buildings and open grounds. From an urban perspective, the compound is a rare "courtyard" in the middle of one of the densest cities in the world. What once stood on the hillside as a prominent symbol of law and order with commanding views to the harbor has now inversely become an urban oasis of openness and calm within a forest of commercial and residential high-rise buildings.

The compound is defined and structured by two large courtyards, known as the Parade Ground and Prison Yard. Herzog & de Meuron's design preserves the openness and distinct character of both courtyards and reactivates them as a new type of urban space for public use. These spaces will define the site physically and programmatically as places of gathering, cultural exchange, leisure, and respite.

Surrounded by several of the site's most historic buildings, the Parade Ground is a formal open area with generous space for public recreation, events, direct access to restaurant and retail attractions, as well as smaller-scale cultural and educational spaces. A new arts and cultural program is one of the key strategies activating the former Prison Yard, transforming it from a rough and foreboding area to a new open public space dedicated to cultural activities.

The former police buildings are gathered mainly at the Lower Courtyard where they sit proudly on the street level or on top of the granite walls, making their authority and presence known. The prison buildings, on the other hand, are located behind the walls, and have historically been separated from public access and view for obvious reasons of safety and security. A new building does not copy either of these historical conditions, but instead creates a new relationship to the context of the site. Conceived as distinctive but carefully inserted elements within the fabric of existing buildings, it is composed of two new volumes that float tightly above the surrounding granite walls. The volumes cantilever above the walls

Tai Kwan Center for Heritage and Art surrounded by Hong Kong's skyscrapers

and maintain a minimum distance to the adjacent structures in order to maximize the buildable floor area while staying within the zoning envelope and creating protective offsets from the surrounding historical buildings. As an architectural expression, it also clearly distinguishes the new buildings from the site's historic buildings.

Elevating the volumes allowed for new public and circulation spaces to be created below. This results in generous protected places for gathering and activity, and establishes a new east-west pedestrian connection from Arbuthnot Road to Old Bailey Street. The buildings also become new markers at the two ends of the compound, bringing attention to a formerly closed-off part of the city.

Courtyard entrance of JC Contemporary

Back-street view of JC Contemporary

North entrance of JC Contemporary

Enclosed interface

The design of JC Contemporary, located at the southwest portion of the site, is developed in close relation to the adaptive reuse of F Hall. New connections are created between the two buildings, which are used for hosting contemporary art functions. The courtyard entrance of JC Contemporary is defined by the building's volume hovering above the historic revetment wall. This entrance area is protected from rain and sun, and acts as the circulation hub and foyer to both F Hall and JC Contemporary. F Hall is a versatile gallery space for art exhibitions and other events. Much of the original architecture, with its traces from the building's past use, is retained and preserved. In contrast, the adjacent JC Contemporary features large column-free exhibition spaces with maximum flexibility, and skylights in the roof provide natural daylight into the top gallery space. The second floor is dedicated to a restaurant with an outdoor terrace overlooking the rich and textured roofscape of the entire compound embedded in the cityscape.

The new JC Cube marks the southeast corner of the site. The volume similarly hovers above the revetment wall along Arbuthnot Road, creating a covered cinema and performance and public gathering space with a large stair that can be used for informal seating. The old D Hall and E Hall prison buildings are to each side of JC Cube, and form interior elevations for the new covered venue. Herzog & de Meuron created two more generous spaces: an 8-meter-high multipurpose space with an accessible technical grid ceiling, and a mechanical plant room that houses cooling towers and equipment serving the entire site.

Internal corridor of an old prison building

Covered cinema and performance and public gathering space

Reinforced-concrete stairwell

Both of JC Contemporary and JC Cube are clad with a cast-aluminum façade system that references the scale and proportion of the existing granite block elements of the revetment wall surrounding the entire site. The 100-percent-recycled-aluminum façade provides a distinctive architectural expression and materiality, distinguishing the buildings as new insertions amid the historical masonry blocks, while also providing structural support, sun shading, and rain protection. The specific porosity, patterning, and expression of the façade units are informed by the functional and environmental requirements of the interior spaces. The materiality of the cast aluminum has a distinctive roughness and texture, which helps to reduce the façade's reflectivity and glare during the day. The units filter the light emitted from the building at night, allowing views of activities taking place within, but reducing levels of light outside.

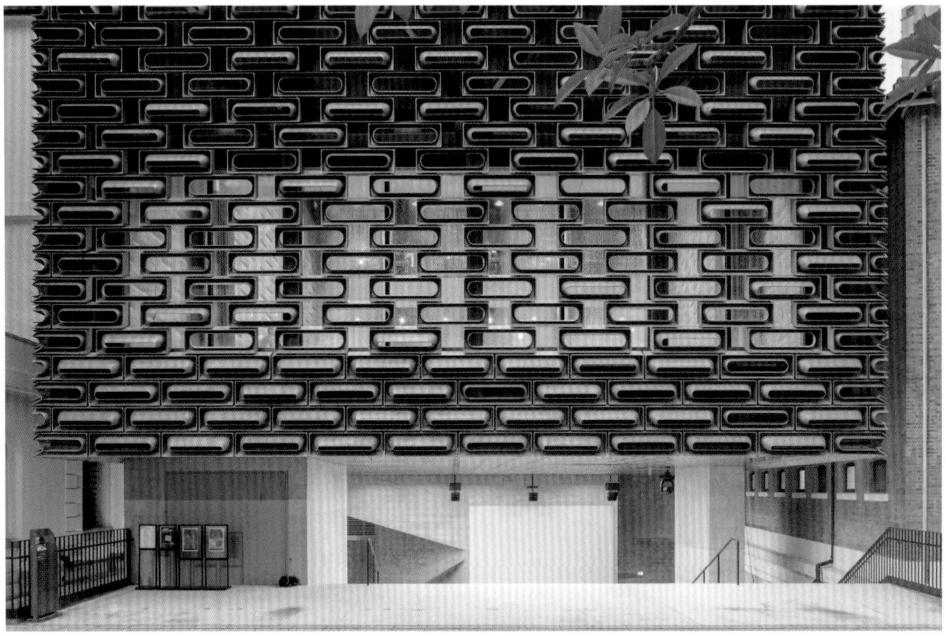

1 1. Entrance of JC Cube
2 2. Cast-aluminum façade system on JC Cube

"What we have done in Hong Kong is to transform a former police station into a center for heritage and arts. In Hong Kong and also in Mainland China this is still a totally new approach to architecture—an unusual thing to do because normally old buildings and entire neighborhoods are being removed and replaced by new ones. The principle is tabula rasa. For us architects, also in the West, it was quite similar until not so long ago.

Modernism was making preexisting things look old, shabby, and uncool. In daily life we all still carelessly throw away things we use every day instead of recycling and reintegrating them in a somewhat appropriate or even creative way. In the 1970s, when we started our practice, we first had to find and define our own architectural language. Reinventing and reusing preexisting ideas and objects—not necessarily of a heroic period of the past, but simply of what we found in front of us—has become an essential element within our vocabulary since those early days and projects. Think of early projects such as Marktplatz in Basel and Stone House in Tavole, and later of course Tate Modern, or now Tai Kwun. We adopted this strategy of working with, instead of against, the existing material world of objects because we found it natural and inspiring, often resulting in unexpected and innovative results.

There is no fundamental difference for such an approach, whether you do it in Basel or in London, in Liguria or in Hong Kong."

Jacques Herzog, July 2018

First-level plan

1. Block 14
2. Block 51 (JC Cube)
3. Block 15
4. Block 50 (JC Contemporary)
5. Block 17
6. Laundry yard
7. Reception
8. Ticketing
9. Lift
10. Lounge
11. Bar area
12. Event space
13. Lobby

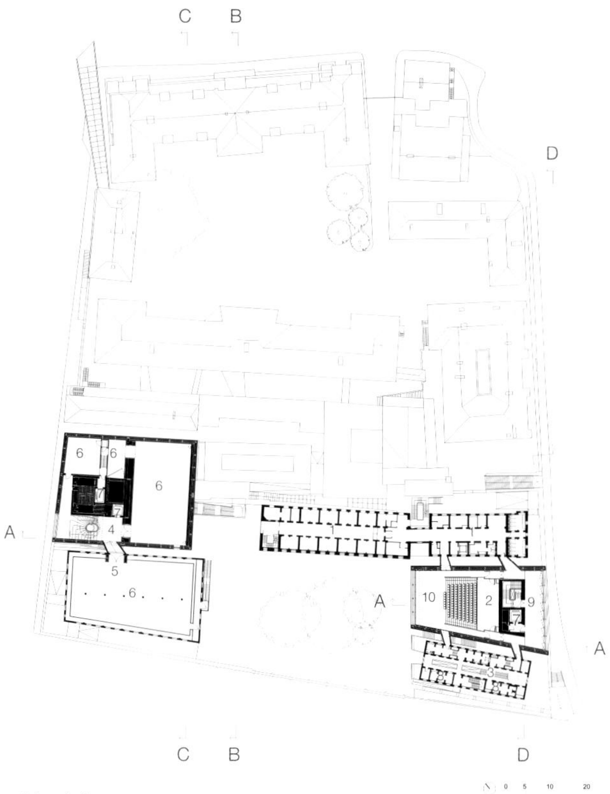

Second-level plan

1. Block 14
2. Block 51 (JC Cube)
3. Block 15
4. Block 50 (JC Contemporary)
5. Block 17
6. Gallery
7. Lift
8. Dressing rooms
9. Foyer
10. Multipurpose hall

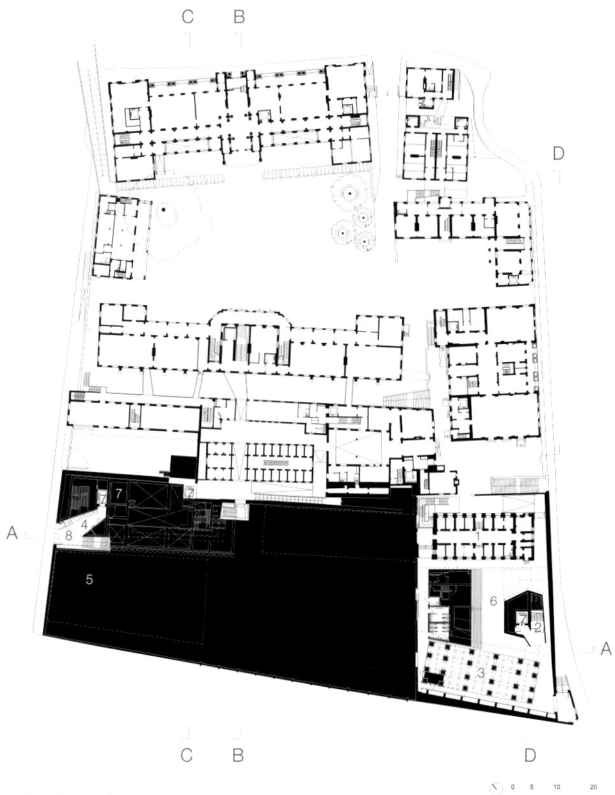

Below-first-level plan

1. Block 14
2. Block 51 (JC Cube)
3. Block 15
4. Block 50 (JC Contemporary)
5. Block 17
6. Laundry yard
7. Lift
8. Lobby

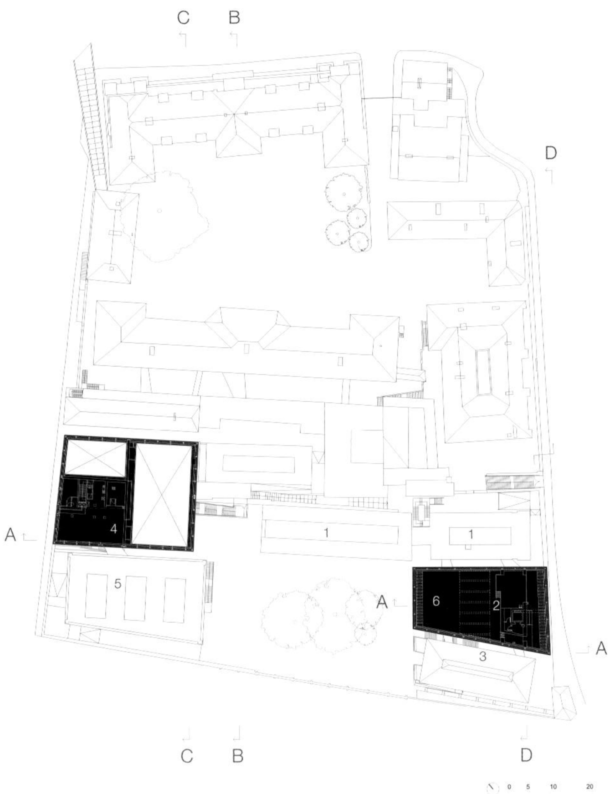

Fifth-level plan

1. Block 14
2. Block 51 (JC Cube)
3. Block 15
4. Block 50 (JC Contemporary)
5. Block 17
6. Technical floor

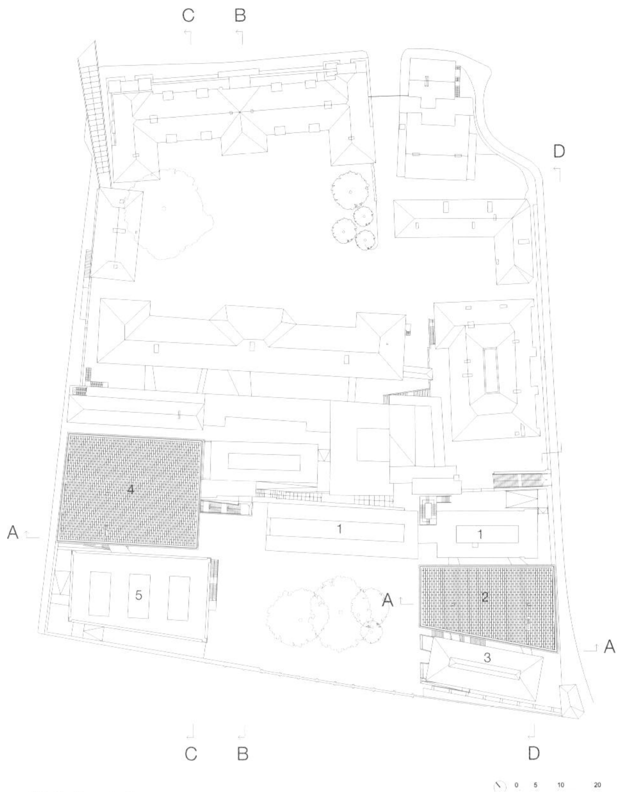

Sixth-level plan

1. Block 14
2. Block 51 (JC Cube)
3. Block 15
4. Block 50 (JC Contemporary)
5. Block 17

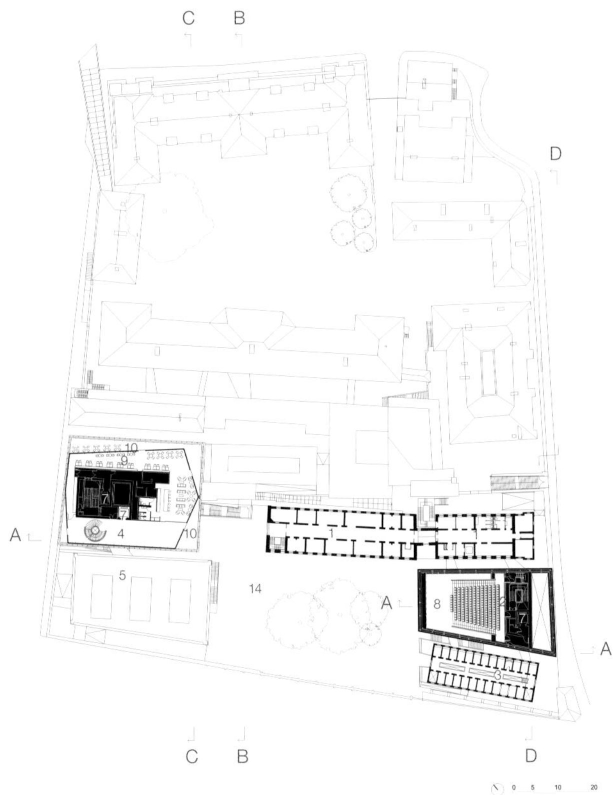

Third-level plan

1. Block 14
2. Block 51 (JC Cube)
3. Block 15
4. Block 50 (JC Contemporary)
5. Block 17
6. Technical floor
7. Lift
8. Multipurpose hall
9. Restaurant
10. Restaurant terrace

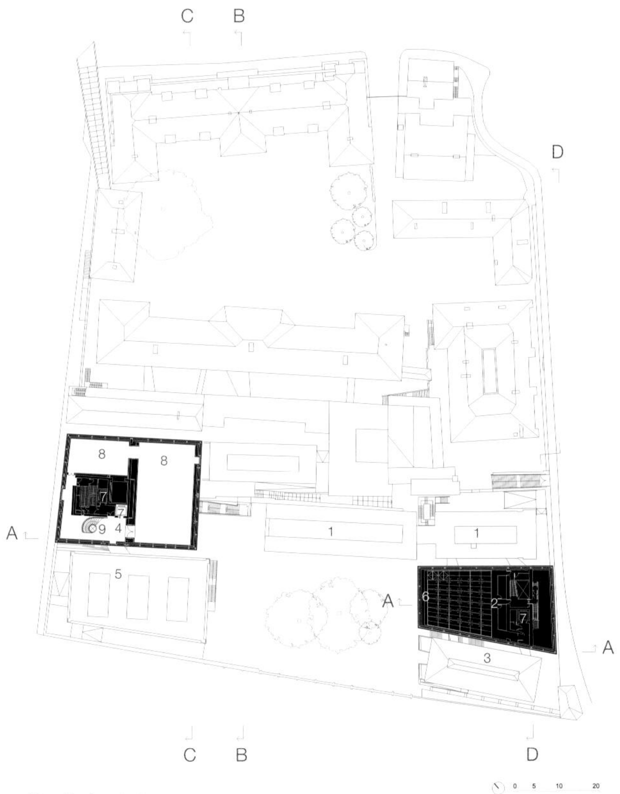

Fourth-level plan

1. Block 14
2. Block 51 (JC Cube)
3. Block 15
4. Block 50 (JC Contemporary)
5. Block 17
6. Technical ceiling
7. Lift
8. Gallery
9. Lobby

West elevation

Section A-A

Section B-B

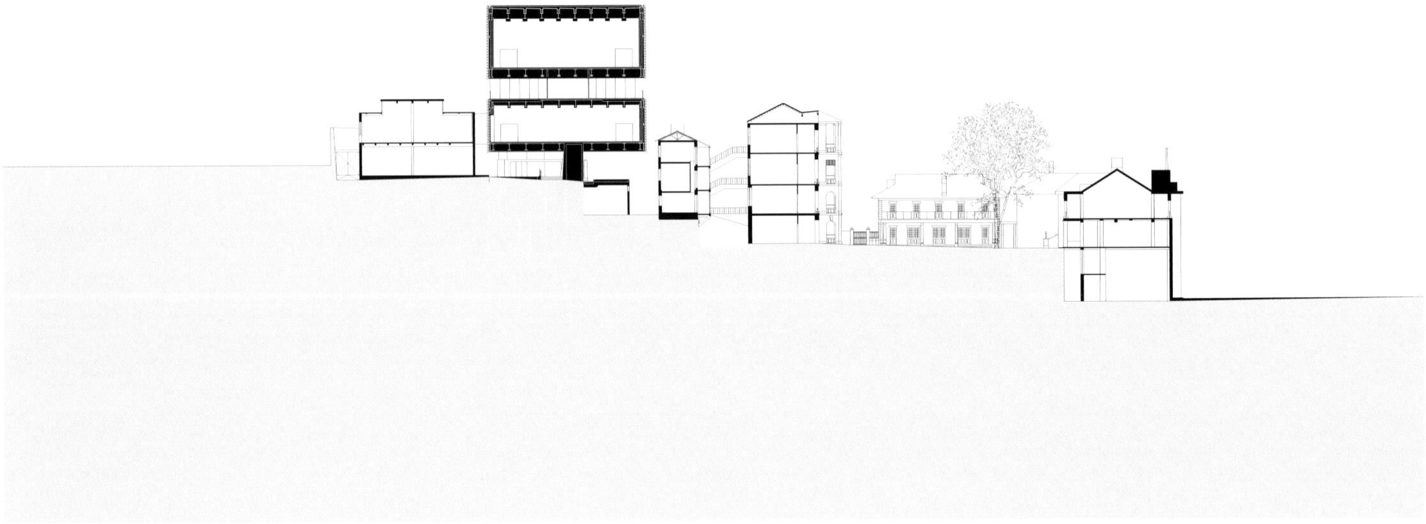

Section C-C

Section D-D

LOST VILLA QINYONG

Atelier XÜK

Location: Qinyong Village, Yinzhou District, Ningbo, Zhejiang Province
Architect: Atelier XÜK
Principal architects: Liu Kenan, Zhang Xu
Design team: Wang Yekai, Huang Jin, He Di, Cai Wuyi, Huang Zirui, Liu Bolun
Area: 1,890 square meters
Design and construction period: March 2018–December 2018
Photography: Chen Hao

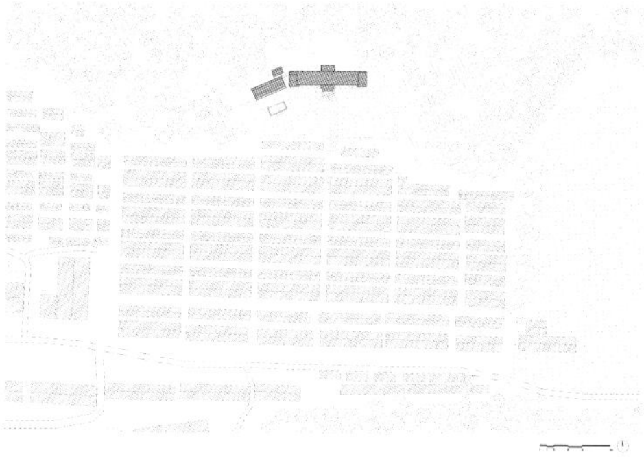

Site plan

Interview with architect Liu Kenan: Strategies of intervention in rural construction

Jiang Jiawei, Liu Kenan

Jiang Jiawei (JJ):

Could you provide a short introduction of how Qinyong Village came to be selected as the site for a Lost Villa boutique hotel?

Liu Kenan (LK):

This village, now called Qinyong, is located on the hillside of Mount Taibai, southeast of Ningbo. The village, which used to be notorious for being a "rotten village" in the 1960s, was transformed under a specific historical circumstance. In response to the central government's call to "learn from Dazhai in agriculture," the former villages of Qinyong and Fengling were merged in the 1970s, and new construction began. It became the first strictly planned rural village in Zhejiang Province. The original natural fabrics and traces were wiped out, and a grid of houses was constructed.

Lost Villa Boutique Hotel overlooking the uniform row houses

View towards the wing building and infinity pool

The entire new village, including the entrance gate, paths, and individual houses, are constructed from drab brown sandstone. The whole village is so homogenized physically and spatially that one can hardly distinguish any differences in building chronology or family relationships. The uniformed row houses were a feature of the people's commune and brought a brand-new appearance to the traditional villages, which have been long governed by the patriarchal clan system. The contemporary primary school, collective canteens, guest houses, and the assembly hall all witness the fiery collectivism of the period. The saying "Learn from Dazhai in agriculture; learn from Qinyong in Zhejiang" is really a high appraisal from the state.

When moving away from the "red" period, the passion in this stone-made village gradually faded, and the public buildings became deserted. In recent years the village administration began developing the unique scenic and cultural resources in order to revitalize this young decaying village. Tourism is brought in, and the public venues of villagers' collective memory, such as the primary school and assembly hall, have become the most important drawcards for tourists. According to the overall planning, the well-preserved masonry structure of the primary school is to be transformed into a boutique hotel. This is the background of how Lost Villa came to Qinyong Village.

JJ:

Were you assigned to any project orientation or design requirements at the beginning of the commission?

LK:

Lost Villa, as the brand name implies, chooses sites that have exquisite scenery and convenient transportation. Normally these are about a half-hour drive from the high-speed train station, aiming to attract guests from first-tier cities. Until now, Lost Villa has opened about 10 branches, most of which are in the south Yangtze River region. Each branch has about 20 guest rooms, which has become somewhat fixed as its common size.

From the operation mode, Lost Villa provides a housekeeping-like service, different from a normal resort hotel. From the aspect of design, it is closer to a boutique hotel. Only a few branches operate like a centralized hotel. More branches have detached buildings and tend to promote one single building for block bookings. What does this mean? The branch sells all four or five rooms of a single building to a group of guests. This mode of selling is suitable for a large family or group of friends, and is also well suited for team building activities of small and medium-sized enterprises.

The situation differs in Qinyong. All the rooms are distributed in a single large block instead of scattered in several detached buildings, so it is not possible to make a block booking. Lost Villa Qinyong is more like a resort hotel, and this was clearly reflected in the design requirements from the client. For example, the client required a large multifunctional hall, which is a standard feature in a normal hotel.

JJ:

Did you do a detailed survey of the site preceding the design?

LK:

I did a basic survey of the village and the site. The context of Qinyong is easier to comprehend, and the design conditions of the site are pretty specific.

Wing building and infinity pool

External corridor

Circulation space

Bridge connecting the main building and wing building

View between the main building and wing building

JJ:
What was your design process?

LK:
I made the decision regarding the general strategy quite quickly, and it was accepted by the client soon thereafter. I immediately proceeded to the spatial arrangement and the design of the form. After the design received approval from the village administrative bureau, it quickly went into construction, even though a certain part of it was still under adjustment. During the construction period I sent a supervisor architect to the site, and I would visit the site every week and a half.

In general, the project pushed forward quickly and smoothly. It consumed my energy only in a few places, for example the cafeteria on the third floor. It took me some time to figure out its unique form.

JJ:
After my site visit, I found the project to be pretty vernacular in the sense that it relates to the adjacent Qinyong Village, instead of to the countryside of Yinzhou or Ningbo or the region of East Zhejiang. This sense of being vernacular comes from your preservation of the original masonry structure of the primary school. Could you explain your design strategy?

LK:
Indeed, my entire idea comes from the preservation of the masonry structure. This was the key point at the start. I prefer to call my design at Qinyong as a strategy of intervention. The original building was made from load-bearing stone masonry walls and prefabricated floor slabs, constituting a structural system that looks like a bookshelf, which in turn determines the system of spatial distribution of the new hotel. The stone blocks are granite from the quarry nearby. In this case, it is impossible to punch into the stone blocks for installing pipelines, and it is also difficult to add new openings in the wall for doors or windows. For economy, there is no choice better than shifting the content of each room. The structure of this bookshelf is obliged to be kept.

There was no fierce intervening action through my design period. I kept almost the entire original stone surface on the main façade and only added new window frames. This stone surface was made in a way that is exactly the same to that in the village. I think this is why you feel it vernacular.

Lobby exterior

JJ:

Was there a structural detection report before your design?

LK:

Yes. The report included the assessment of whether it is possible to turn the original classrooms into guest rooms, and of adding a cafeteria on the roof of the wing building.

JJ:

The cafeteria is the largest new addition in the project. How did you conceive the design?

Cafeteria interior

LK:

Since the masonry walls have to be kept, the skeleton of the primary school can't provide a large enough place for a banquet or party. I took advantage of the resilience of the original masonry structure and placed the cafeteria on the top of the wing building. So, enough room is achieved. The kitchen is inserted into an isolated box structure beside the wing building, and food is served through a dumbwaiter.

The steel structure of the new addition is made with welded square tubes 1.96 inches (5 centimeters) along each edge. The material and its size are the outcome of optimized conditions. Firstly, such a light steel structure makes it possible to transport and install the components by human labor. Secondly, the cross section of the square is preconditioned to hide the steel structure behind the wooden envelop enclosure. In this way, the perception of the warm-toned interior is not disturbed.

After deciding upon the building system, I designed the detailed built form, which was a comprehensive result of the interior experience, the thermal performance of materials, and the consideration of contingency due to the fluctuating quality in rural construction. This can be seen clearly in the southern part of the roof. To respond to the aforementioned requirements, two sunshade panels are suspended from above, and they make a contribution to the interior experience of the large-scaled landscape through a borrowing and blocking of scenery. The sunshade panels on the south side reduce the solar radiation as well as the energy consumption in air conditioning. They also lower the sightline of guests to the eave, and in this way the view of scenery is framed. Skylights are used in the northern part of the roof, and they frame the scenery of the tree crown to the north of the hotel. Taking account of the insufficiency of the rural technique in bringing a complete waterproofness to these skylights, I added sunshade panels, which might help protect against rain and falling leaves.

Landscaping in front of the building

JJ:

An infinity pool is designed in front of the wing building. What was your strategy for integrating the configuration and height of the pool into the landscape design?

LK:

The field to the south of the hotel used to be the primary school playground, and was also used by villagers to grow vegetables. It was retrieved by the village administration after the approval of the boutique hotel project. In order to lower the budget, the client did not commission a landscape office, and thus appointed my studio to do the job. My basic strategy was to keep the original farm field and turn it into a kind of agricultural landscape with terrains of different levels.

After turning in through the village, guests approach the hotel by stone steps. They ascend about 3 meters to arrive at the terrain. It is the first moment they catch sight of the entire south façade—an impressive monolithic block of masonry under the sun. They proceed into the lobby, and the impression changes with the circulation and usage of space. After the renovation, it is no longer possible to convey the monolithic feeling of the structure in the guest rooms. So it became essential for me to maintain a flat terrain to show the monolithic block to the guests.

The infinity pool is more like an outcome of technology. Normally such a pool needs a pump room, which in this case is inserted beneath the pool. The total height of the pool and the pump room precisely meets the elevation difference of the original playground and the primary school building. Following this idea, I embedded the water circulation system in the assembled components, which are all made by granite plaster.

Rear of the building

Internal corridors in the main building

JJ:

Have you kept the preliminary sketches? I wonder if there is any specific trace of design.

LK:

It is a pity that there are hardly any sketches left now. But actually, I did not rely on making sketches to push my design. It was more like a process of filtering out the options that did not fit my design philosophy, the programming, and the budget. The final built form was attained gradually through the construction process instead of by a decided shape after rounds of sketches.

JJ:

What are some keywords that conclude your design strategy for this project?

LK:

I find it dangerous to make a mere conclusion to a design. I do not mean that keywords are of no use, but it does confuse readers if such keywords are discussed without context.

Since I do need to give an answer, I would prefer to mention "bricolage"—a key concept from the book *La Pensée Sauvage* [*The Savage Mind* (1962)]. The difference of a bricoleur and an engineer, according to Claude Lévi-Strauss, remains among the concrete and the abstract science.

I find that it applies to the circumstance of rural construction in China. It is not difficult to adopt the idea of bricolage to elaborate my modus operandi in the Qinyong project. A bricoleur does their job by using tools at hand. This is different from an engineer, who relies heavily on the materials and instruments of a systemized design. The tool kit world of a bricoleur is closed, and their fundamental modus operandi is to collect as many objet trouvés as possible. In other words, a bricoleur owns a certain set of tools and materials of a closed world, and they are selected to solve a certain problem in a given task. It turns out to be a result of contingency based on what has happened.

All the modus operandi in my design are not a priori. Instead, they are a positive response to the specific demand to control costs. The limited budget hardly supports the purchase of high-quality windows and doors as well as well-designed furniture. I would rather seek a way towards an integrated design than purchasing imitation products. A special experience of the interior is thus brought in by this idea.

The concept of intervention that I mentioned before is another keyword.

Roof terrace connecting to the cafeteria

JJ:

I find it appropriate to use the word intervention to describe Lost Villa Qinyong. As a renovation project, it does not provide the luxury of a normal five-star hotel. Have you used the similar modus operandi in your other recent projects?

LK:

The strategy of intervention plays a fundamental role in the Qinyong project, which has a set of relatively clear design demands. A common point in my recent projects is that spatial elements such as closets, restrooms, and locker rooms are embedded in the interior as cubes. Since the materials they use are different from those in other parts of the interior, some conventional life experiences might thus be differentiated. Such can be apprehended as an intervention of contemporary life.

Framed view of the hill behind

View from the cafeteria

Staircase details

JJ:

Your strategy of the cube deserves research. I notice that you have not made any of your projects into a "white box." What do you think about this type of cube?

LK:

Indeed, I have not designed any "white box" projects, and I don't think I will do so in the future. In my view, the white box expresses abstract space, which is a result of dematerialization. It does not coordinate with my design concept. I have no interest in dematerialization.

JJ:

It seems that you have adopted a design method of "box within box" in some parts of your projects. Have you ever thought about turning your "boxes" into an industrialized and prefabricated product?

LK:

No. For example, in the Qinyong project, even though I made these cubes into prefabricated products, it was not possible to move them into the guest rooms. They were all made on site by carpenters and masons. It took a lot of energy for me and my assistants to supervise the site. The nuance among the cubes in different guest rooms is decided by site conditions.

I have not been chasing industrialization and productization in past years. I mention the concept of bricolage because it provides another path of thinking parallel to industry. The design potentiality in my conception of cubes is a means rather than an end.

Raised platform in a guest room

JJ:

You did frequently mention the term bricolage in your recent lectures. However, generally speaking a boutique hotel is not willing to rely on such a strategy, which can seem to be a makeshift measure. How did you break through this barrier?

LK:

A boutique hotel conventionally indicates something related to being of high quality. Yet high quality resides in a way that provides psychological relief from daily life, rather than in the exquisiteness of built details. A boutique hotel in the modern conception should bring in new experiences for its guests, instead of providing on-call service or a space made by expensive building materials. The average price of Lost Villa is around 1,000 renminbi per room per night, which is equal to that of a luxury hotel in the city. If a guest spends 40 minutes driving from the Ningbo high-speed train station to this hotel in Qinyong, they are not looking for an experience similar to an urban luxury hotel.

In the Qinyong project, the use of interior materials enhances integration, and provides a sense of make-do in certain parts. Furnishings are a familiar scale but not ordinary, as they are made by carpenters instead of cabinetmakers. This can be seen in my use of railings, for example. Metal railings are put in the place where wainscoting panels used to be, and TV benches are also designed with railings together. Each bed is divided into two parts. The main body is movable, and the headboard is combined with railings. It brings in an experience of defamiliarization, which helps guests enjoy a moment of relaxation.

I attempted to break the boundary between the division of architectural design, interior decoration, and soft furnishings. By integrating them I distinguish the Lost Villa boutique hotel from normal luxury hotels in the city. It aims at creating an atmosphere of the countryside, which meets the imagination of urban dwellers.

JJ:

How did you realize these ideas?

LK:

A raised platform became a driving force throughout my design, under the control of the strategy of intervention. Made with wood, this platform extends all around the guest rooms and corridors and plays a mediating role. Firstly, it makes enough room for pipeline facilities, which used to be hidden above the suspended ceiling. Secondly, it helps avoid the risk of drilling holes in the masonry walls. Through this continuous raised platform, the pipeline facilities are connected, and the freedom of interior distribution is achieved.

At the same time, the raised platform also responds to the scale of the guest room. The original height of the classroom was too high for a guest room, so the raised platform creates a better interior feeling. Also, the homogenizing character of the platform reveals a sense of uncommonness within the conventional building materials. This is exactly my specific modus operandi to bring in new experiences.

Lobby interior

Guest room interior

New external corridor

JJ:

How did you handle materials in the Qinyong project?

LK:

In the Qinyong project, the wooden frame serves as the main body of the carpentry. Wood is used for architectural elements almost everywhere in the lobby and locker rooms, as well as the envelope enclosure in the bathrooms. It is also adopted in the furniture, such as air-conditioning cabinets and interior railing panels.

JJ:

From my own observation, the carpentry system in your projects enhances the tolerance of on-site rural construction.

LK:

I agree. Enhancing the tolerance helps me respond to the thorny problems in rural construction, such as lack of accuracy, difficulties in communication, and so on. The built effect of all my current works in the rural context is a result of tolerance.

JJ:

Thank you for the interview.

External staircase

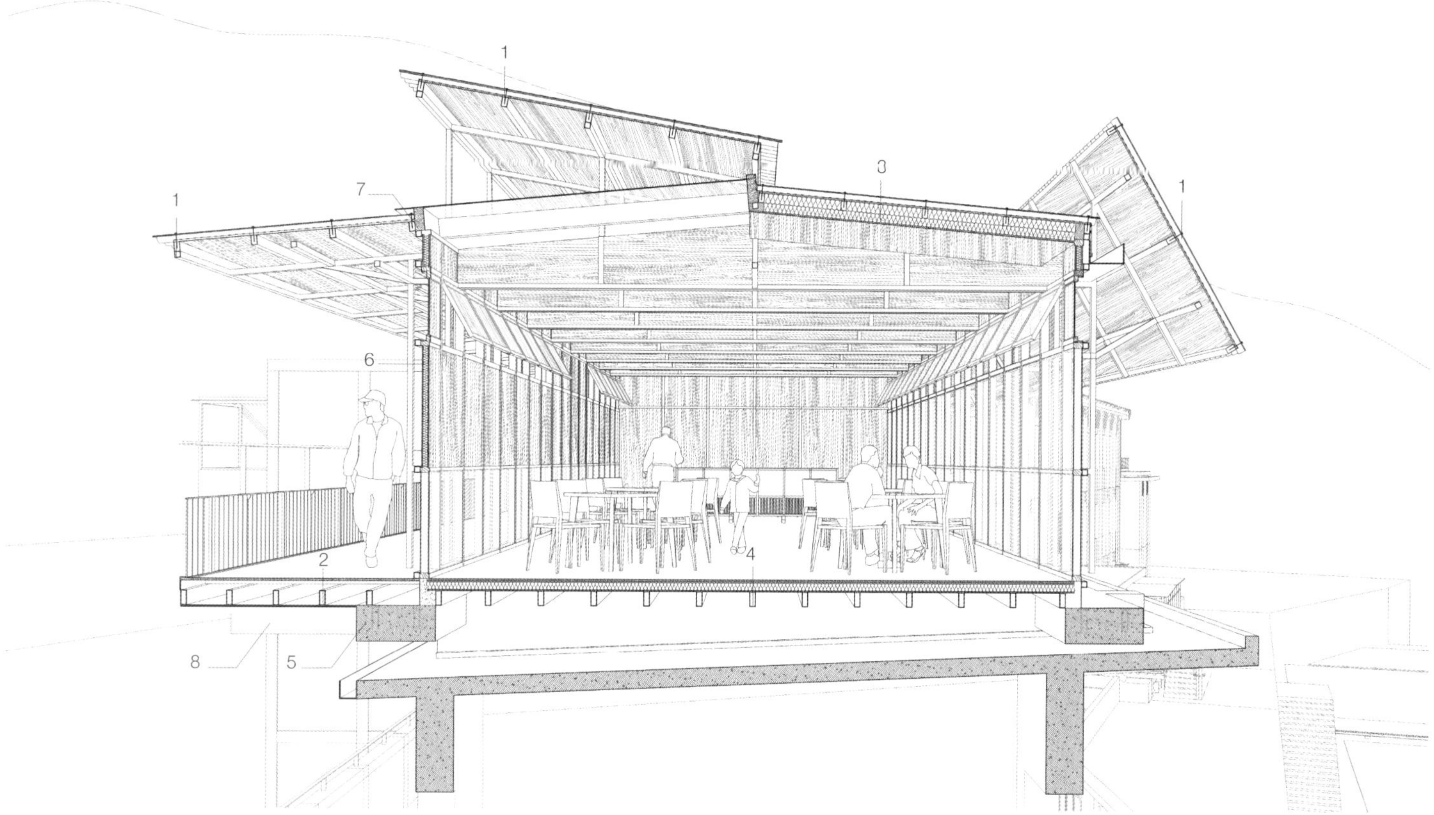

Perspective section of the cafeteria

1, 3. Corrugated cement fiber roofing panel fixed onto steel
2. Preservative-treated timber floor
4. Composite wood floor
5. In-situ reinforced-concrete slab
6. Pine wood veneer fixed in wood frame
7. Pine wood skylight frame
8. In-situ reinforced-concrete beam

Cafeteria

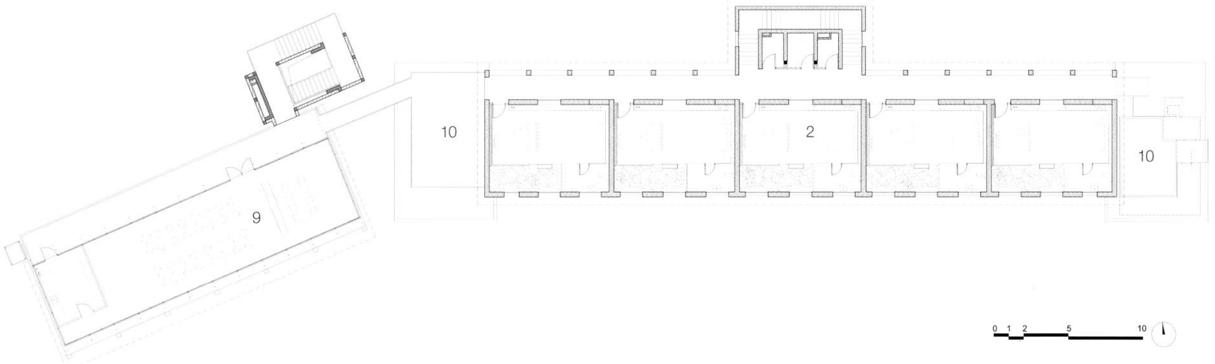

Third-floor plan

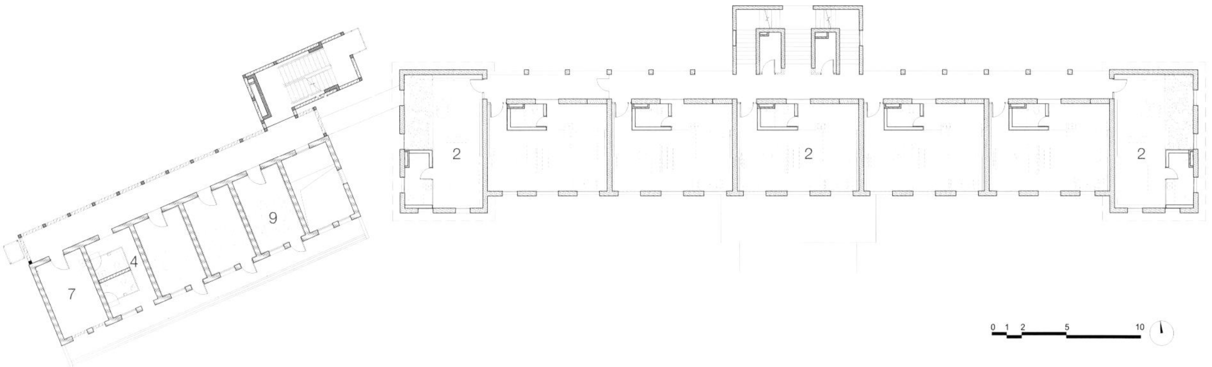

Second-floor plan

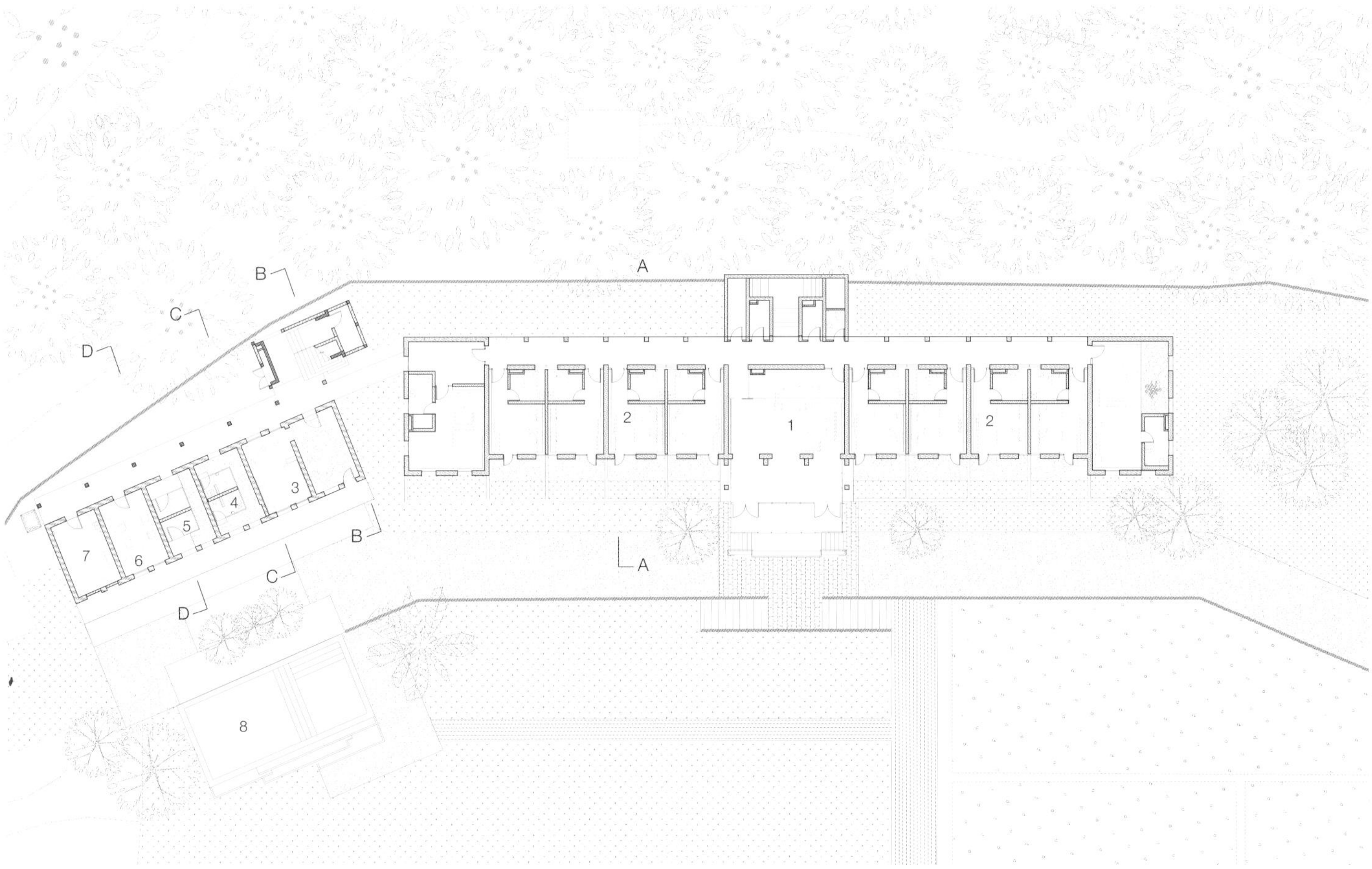

First-floor plan

1. Lobby
2. Guest room
3. Water bar
4. Restroom
5. Locker room
6. Office
7. Storage
8. Infinity pool
9. Cafeteria
10. Roof terrace

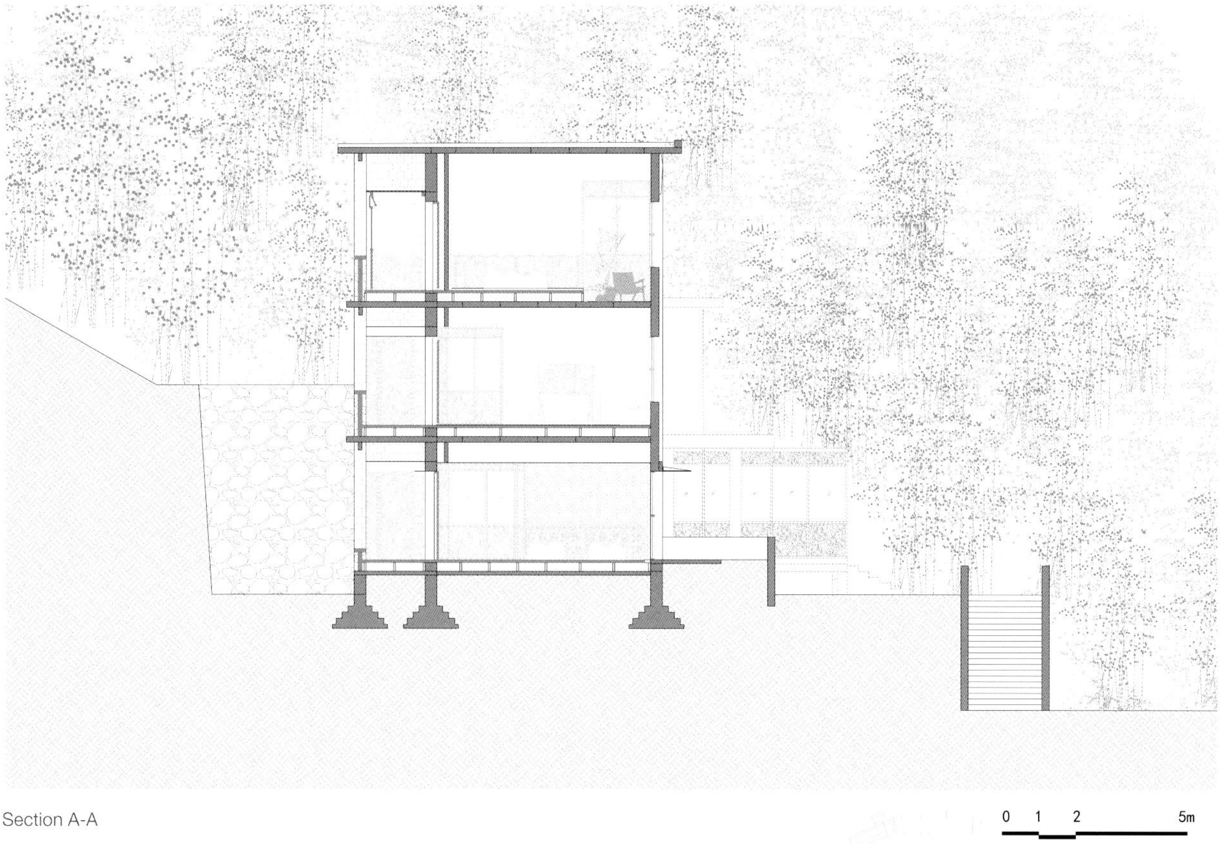

Section A-A

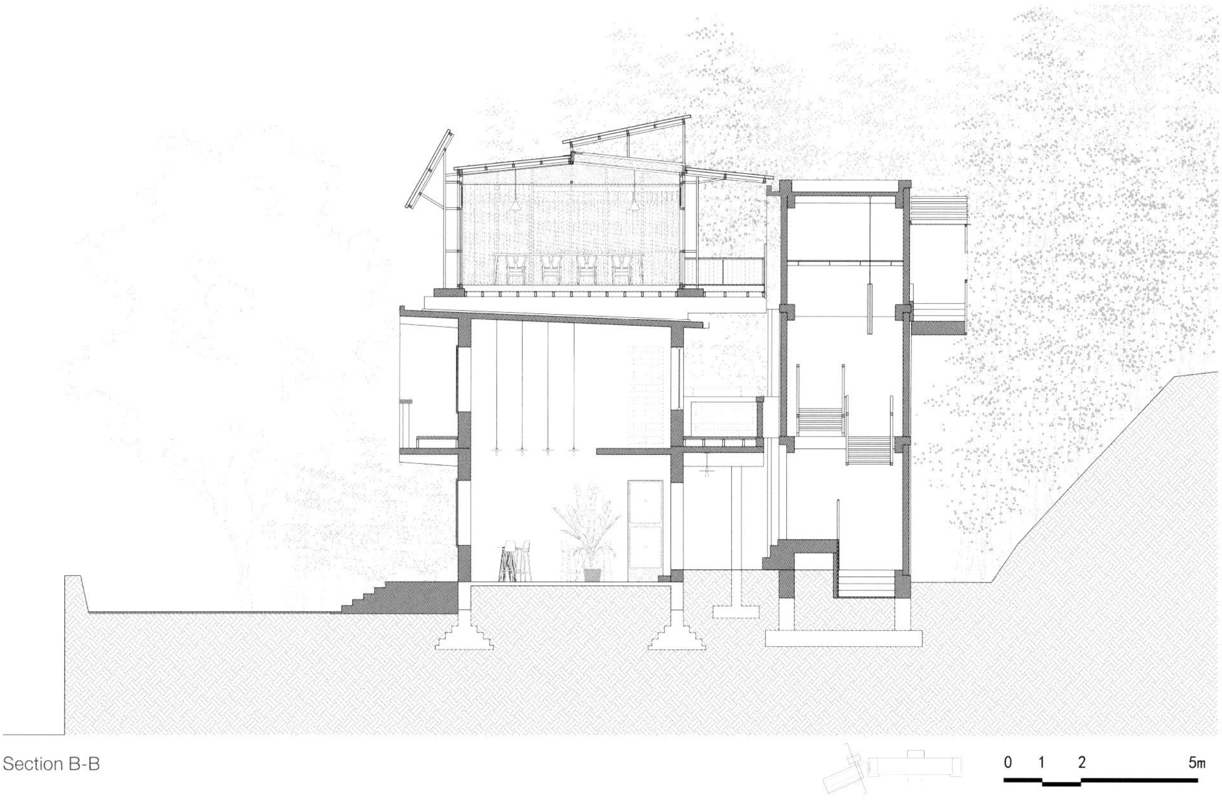

Section B-B

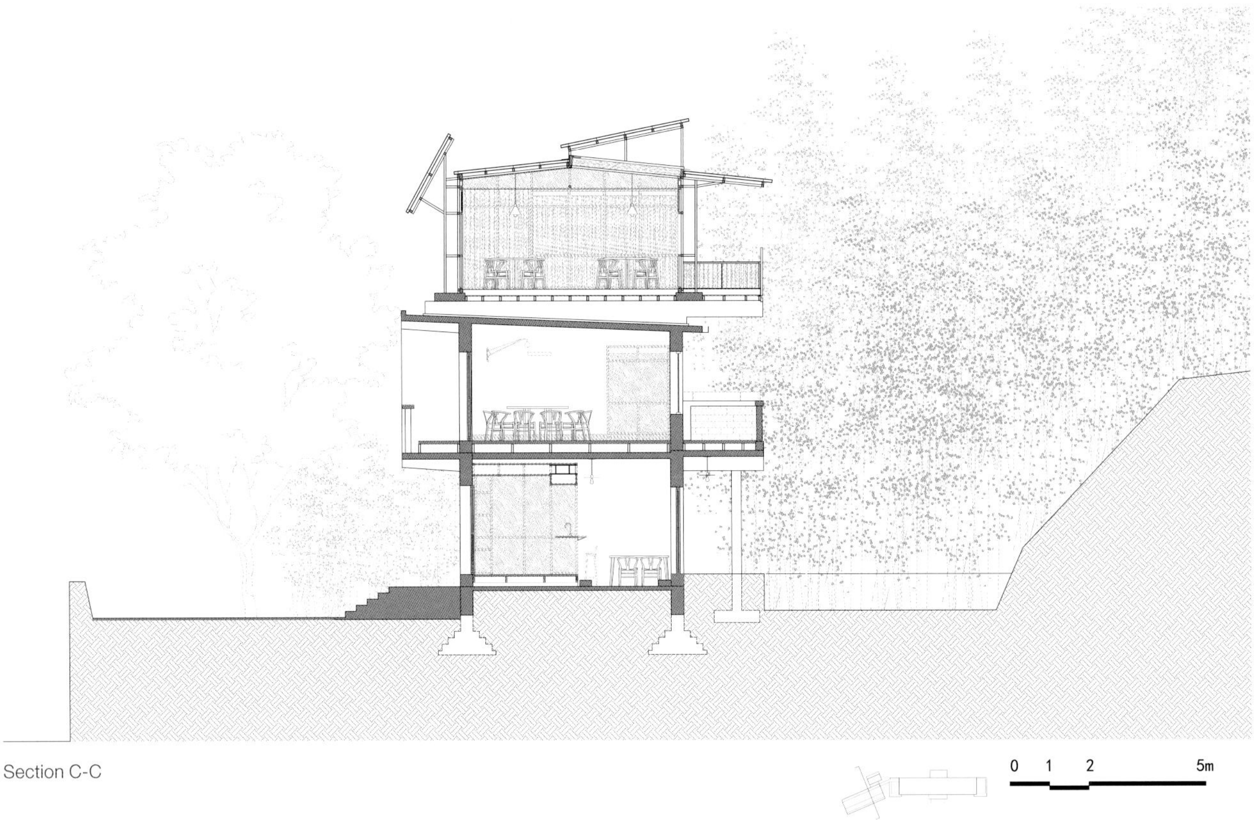

Section C-C

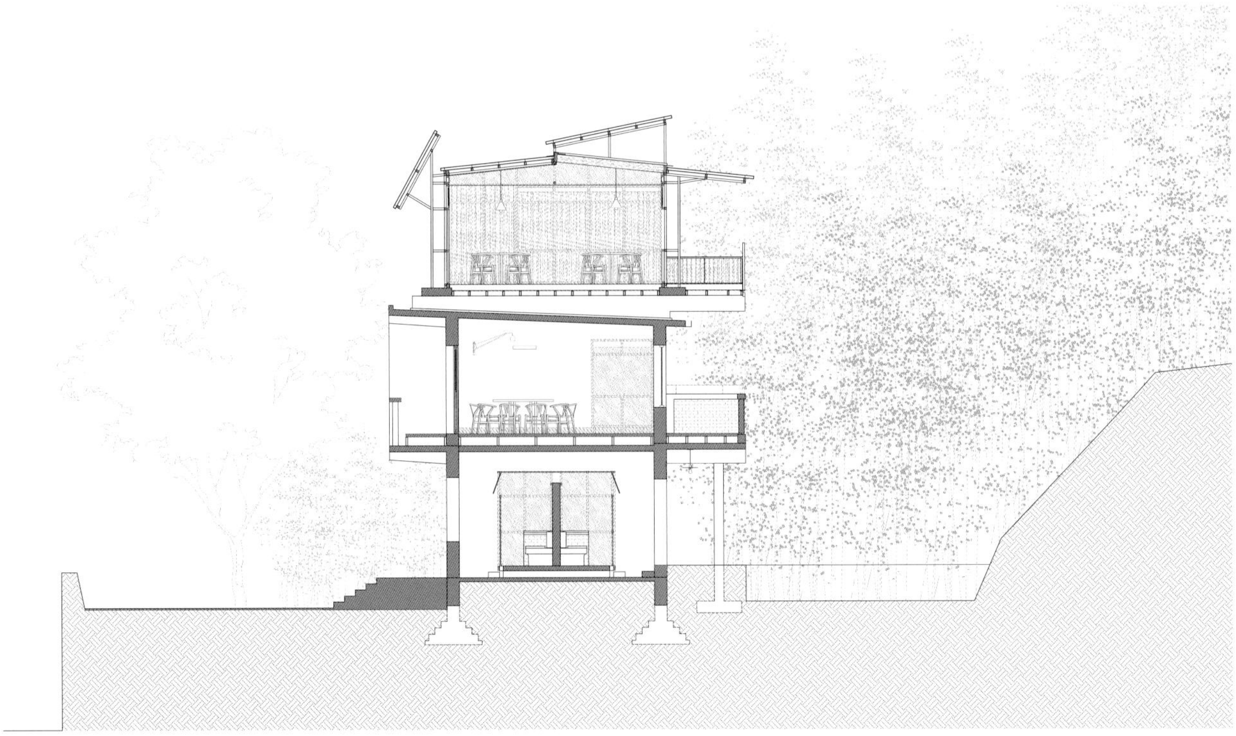

Section D-D

BINGDING WOOD KILN

AZL Architects

Location: Qiancheng Village, Jingdezhen, Jiangxi Province
Architect: AZL Architects
Principal architect: Zhang Lei
Design team: Zhang Xue
Collaboration: Jingdezhen Research Institute of Ceramic Industrial Design
Area: 1,800 square meters
Design and construction period: 2017–2018
Photography: Yao Li, Dong Suhong

The county of Fuliang was once under the administrative jurisdiction of Jingdezhen. It is known as the "Porcelain Capital" of China, and the ancient ruins of Gaoling Mine in Fuliang is a holy place for international ceramics culture. BingDing Wood Kiln is located in Qiancheng Village in Fuliang, less than an hour's drive from the urban area of Jingdezhen. The site is a tranquil environment surrounded by mountains and bamboo forests.

BingDing Wood Kiln surrounded by forest

Entrance and front elevation

The wood kiln is named after the locals' preference of using the Chinese horsetail pine, or red pine, as a form of fuel, and has been the symbol of the industry for nearly 2,000 years. Like any traditional craftsmanship that has survived for more than a millennium, it is suffering from the impact of modern technology and new methods of firing. The development of the wood kiln has been hindered due to the difficulty in controlling the wood consumption and firing effects. In recent years, the wood kiln has faced the threat of extinction because of the widespread adoption of coal and natural gas fuels in newer industrial technologies, as well as the impact of environmental protection requirements. At present, the construction technology for Jingdezhen's egg-shaped wood kiln is only known by 70-year-old Yu Hezhu and his handful of apprentices. This gives rise to the threat that the construction technology may be abandoned.

As a practitioner zealously interested in revitalizing the traditional kiln, the project owner, Mr. Yu, began to learn from the 83-year-old master Yu Xunquan in 2012 for kiln calcining. He then studied under the tutelage of the local area's only successor of the wood kiln technique, Yu Hezhu, in 2014. BingDing Wood Kiln is the masterpiece Mr. Yu completed with his teacher, Yu Hezhu. The construction of the complex double-curved brick arch can only be based on experience. There are no blueprints for reference, nor are there any known written documents.

Entrance detail

Main entrance

BingDing Wood Kiln consists of the building and the kiln. The design revolves around the kiln as the core, coupled with the configuration of the streamlined and parallel production axis and observation axis. The kiln building adopts a concrete arch similar to the kiln's brick arch structure, and stresses the axial symmetry of the east and west of the kiln. The top light belts, wall windows, and vertical floor joints of the kiln building are all directed to the central axis of the kiln.

The production lines of the kiln building are mainly located on the first floor, including the front platform of the kiln and the steps on the two sides of the stairs, which are largely used during kiln filling, calcining, and opening. The rooms near the exterior windows on the two sides of the first floor are used for daily work such as glazing, molding, polishing, enameling, saggaring, and storing porcelain. More than 30 kiln workers are on site day and night. Their temporary living space is behind the kiln.

Torch lighting ceremony in the inner space

Kiln at the core of the interior

Lattice inlaid bricks in the arched exterior openings

Concrete arches of the building are similar to the kiln's arched brick structure

Stairs used during kiln filling, calcining, and opening

The concrete formwork is supported by steel structures outside the concrete form for casting, rather than being fixed by ordinary mounting bolts. In addition to the fair-faced concrete, the main material of BingDing Wood Kiln is the bricks of the kiln. The lattice inlaid bricks in the arched window openings above the second floor form patterns of light and shadow cross the interior.

Mr. Yu and the local government hopes the BingDing Wood Kiln will bring more attention to the Jingdezhen ceramic industry and new opportunities for rural craftsmanship inheritance and economic development, as well as the revival of the wood kiln. In Chinese culture, porcelain has always been more than a necessity for daily life. It is also an important container for the sentiments in life.

Concrete arches around the kiln

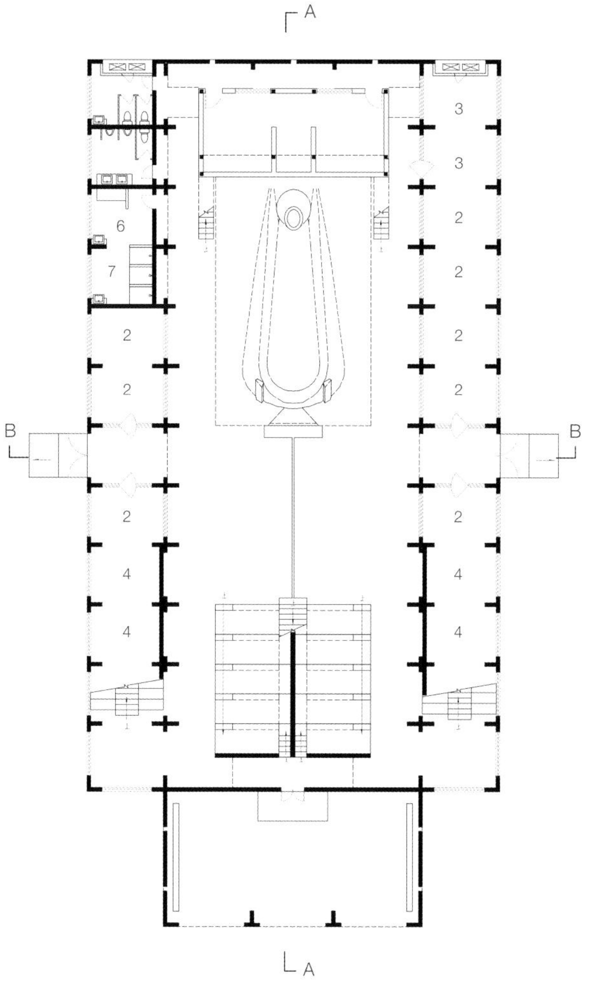

First-floor plan

0 2 4 10m

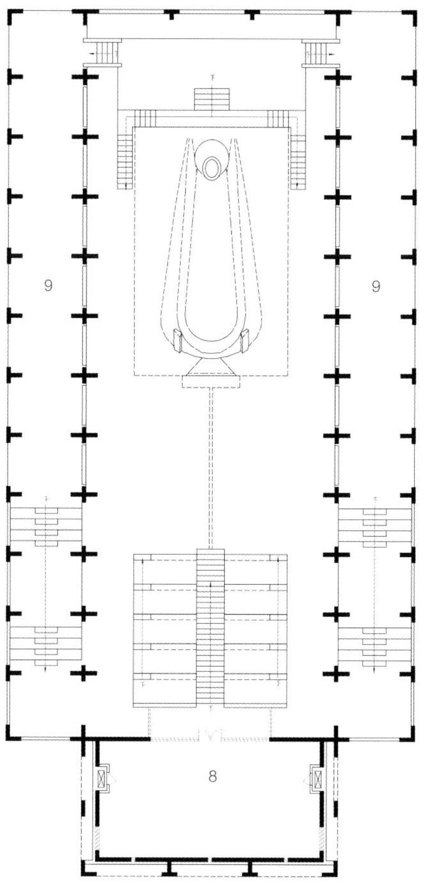

Second-floor plan

0 2 4 10m

1. Wood kiln
2. Loading area
3. Milling area
4. Storage
5. Lounge
6. Locker room
7. Shower room
8. VIP room
9. Exhibition area

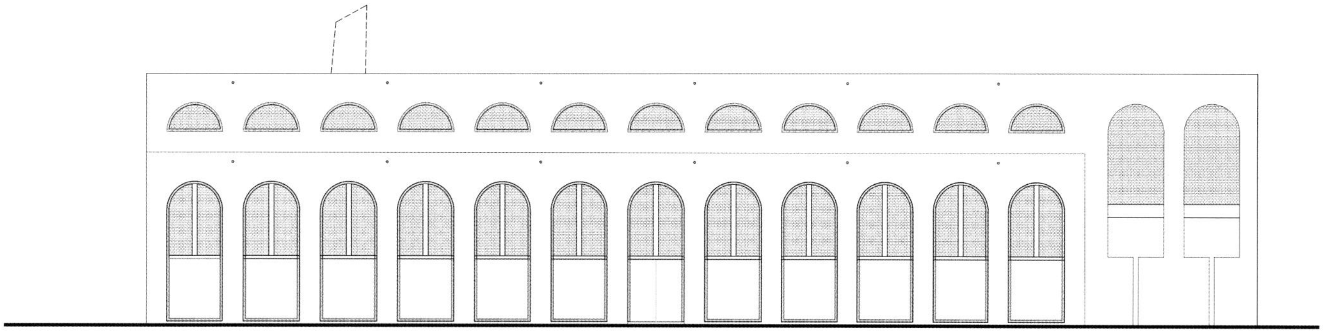

West elevation

0 2 4 10m

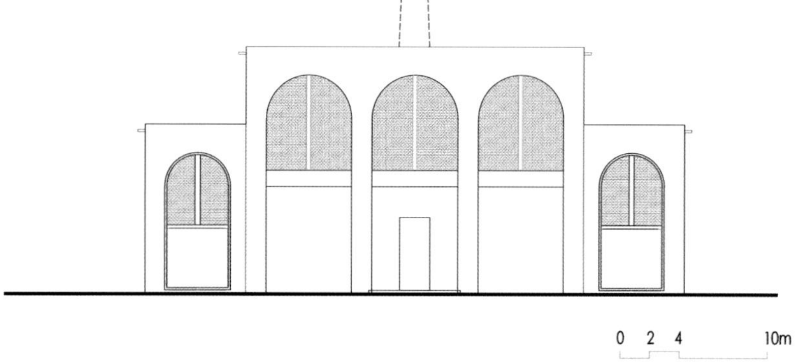

South elevation

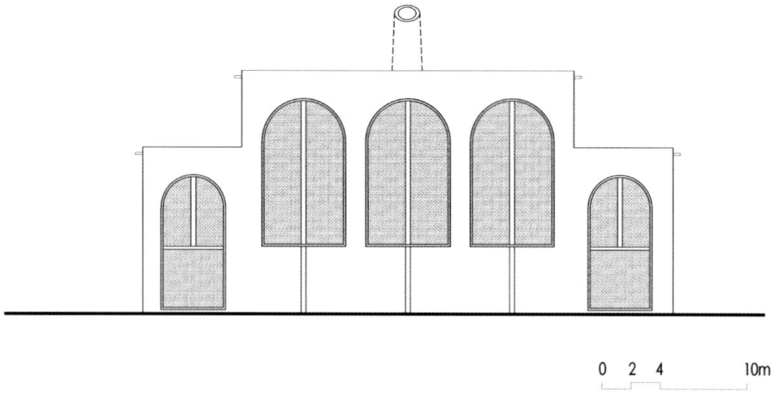

North elevation

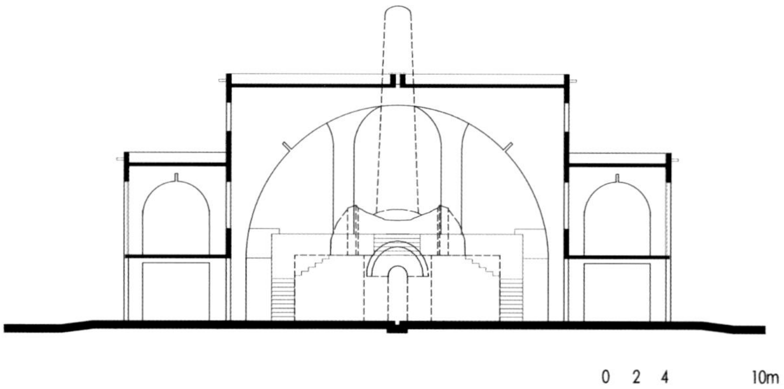

Section B-B

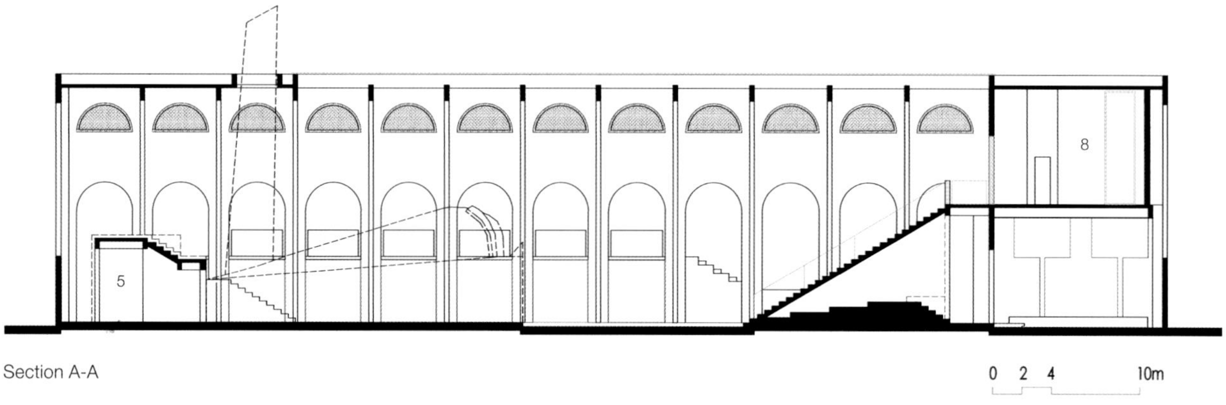

Section A-A

5. Lounge
8. VIP room

NEW BUND DISTRICT CHURCH

Ábalos + Sentkiewicz

Location: Pudong, Shanghai
Architect: Ábalos + Sentkiewicz
Principal architects: Iñaki Ábalos, Renata Sentkiewicz
Design team: Adrian Úbeda, Álvaro Maján, Alexander Jacobson, Eva Castiñeira, Alejandra Salvador, Chen Hao, Hu Chenchen, Teresa Casbas, Wang Yiqun
Collaboration: Pudong Design Institute
Area: 2,837 square meters
Project completion: 2018
Photography: Zhang Yong

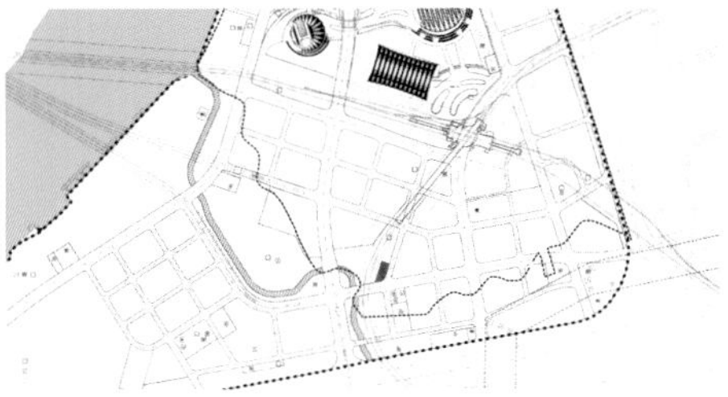

Site plan

The location of the site of New Bund District Church—at the entrance of the New Bund International Business District in Pudong, Shanghai—provided a conflictive situation between the ecclesiastical authorities and the local government, which contacted Ábalos + Sentkiewicz to find a satisfactory solution. The project presented by the church administration did not match the expectations of the Pudong authorities, who expected a church reflecting the modern and cosmopolitan nature of the new development. In addition, the underground infrastructure of the subway constrained construction against the access road to New Bund, resulting in a longitudinal building that sits between the new urban development and the linear park of Huangpu River .

New Bund District Church as a gateway to the park

New Bund District Church at the corner of two main streets

The configuration of the building unifies the design of the religious and administrative functions into a single volume that functions as a gateway to the park, an open-air meeting space, an urban landmark, and a privileged viewpoint of the surroundings.

The roof is conceived as an extension of the park, and in the manner of European cathedrals with accessible roofs. A picturesque public stairway, which turns towards the front of the church, ascends to the roof of the building—a natural belvedere above the park and Huangpu River that allows the gathering of the community for outdoor ceremonies.

View from the park

External staircase to entrance

Main entrance

Green rooftop

Main chapel

Main chapel with double-height ceiling

Office area

Gallery of the main chapel

The symbolic character of the main chapel in the central interior space is emphasized as a meeting place for the community. It integrates two types of worship spaces: the longitudinal nave of the Catholic tradition and the Protestant auditorium chapels, conceived around the acoustic, symbolic, and ceremonial role of the choir. A smaller chapel located behind the rear bleacher is separated from the main nave by a mobile wooden wall that can be folded to increase the capacity of the church.

A tight budget restricted materiality to the extensive use of white plaster, and to the use of concrete for the base, bell, and ceiling above the main nave. The strategic and precise use of purely architectural resources, such as natural light, compensates for this limitation on materials. The natural light filters into the interior of the church with a specific intentionality according to each of the orientations.

View across the water

View across the park

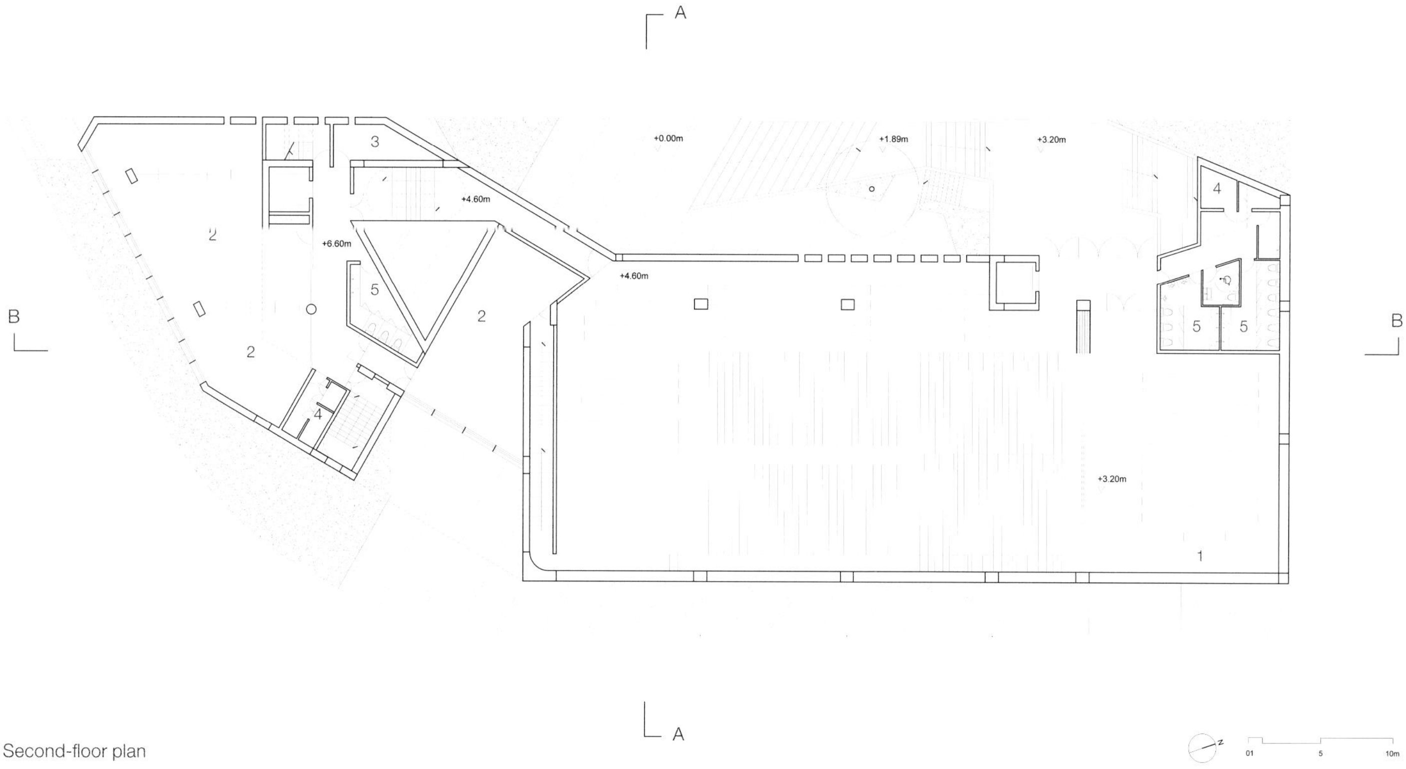

Second-floor plan

1. Main chapel
2. Office
3. VRF
4. Power distribution room
5. Restroom

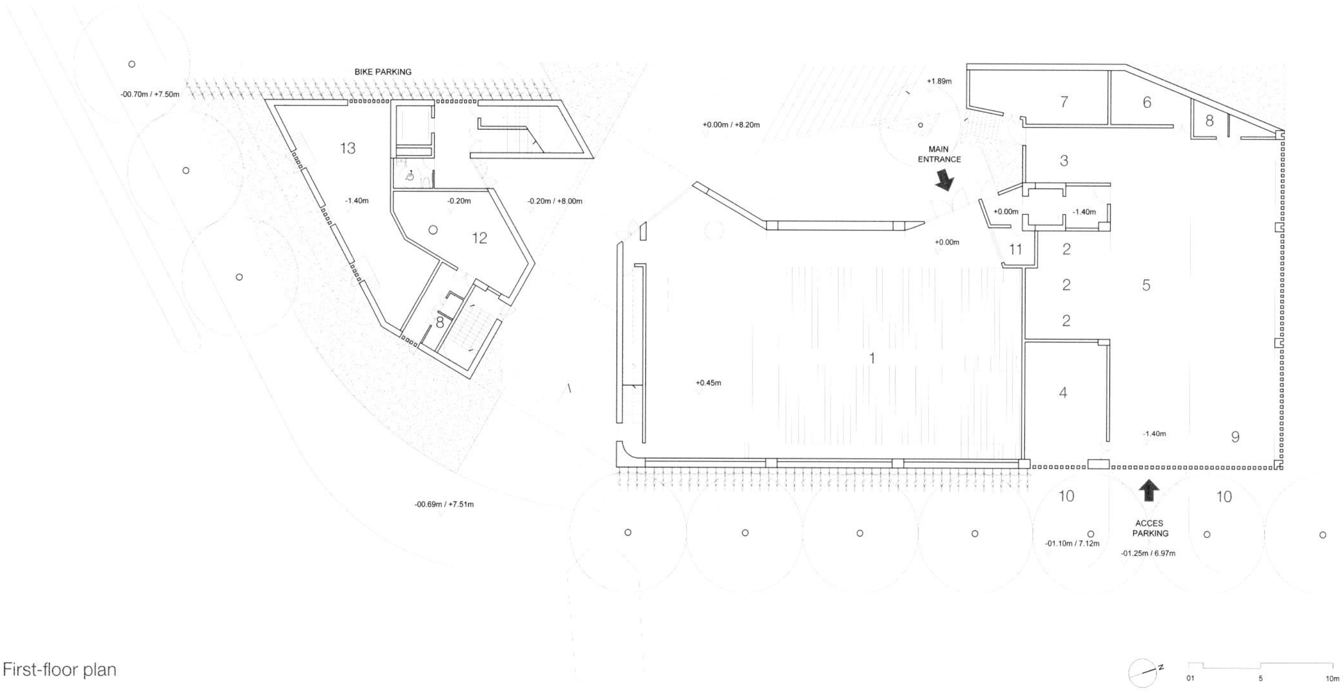

First-floor plan

1. Main chapel
2. Spot with electricity
3. Seating for people with a disability
4. Air-conditioning plant
5. Parking
6. Comunication room
7. Fire control room
8. Power distribution room
9. Parking
10. Parking
11. Acoustic control
12. Pump room
13. Substation

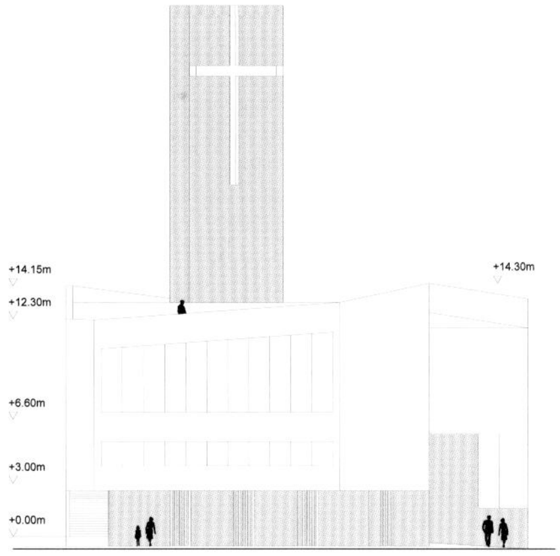

South elevation

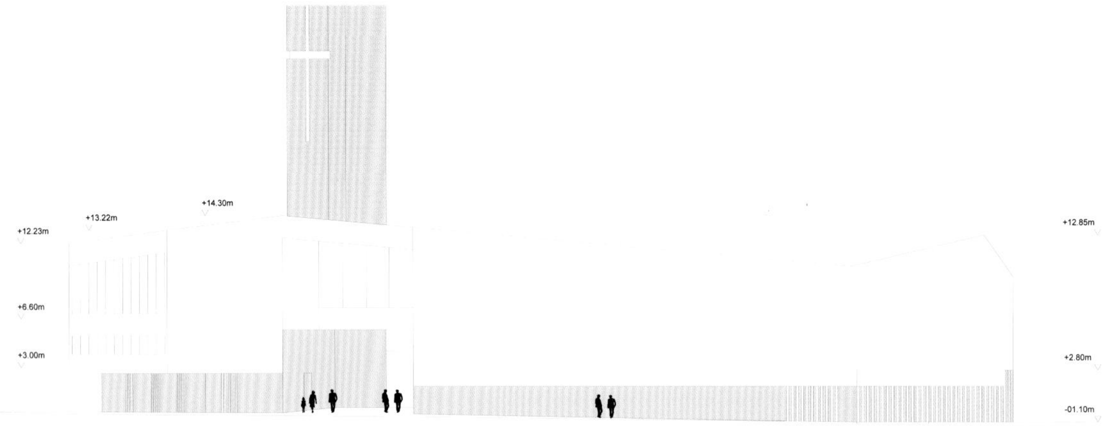

East elevation

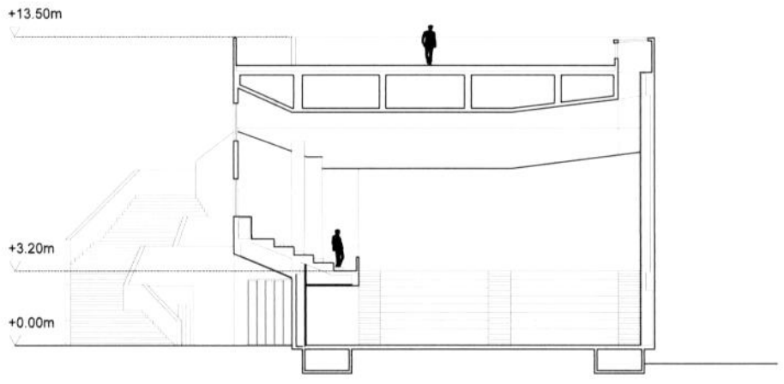

Section A-A

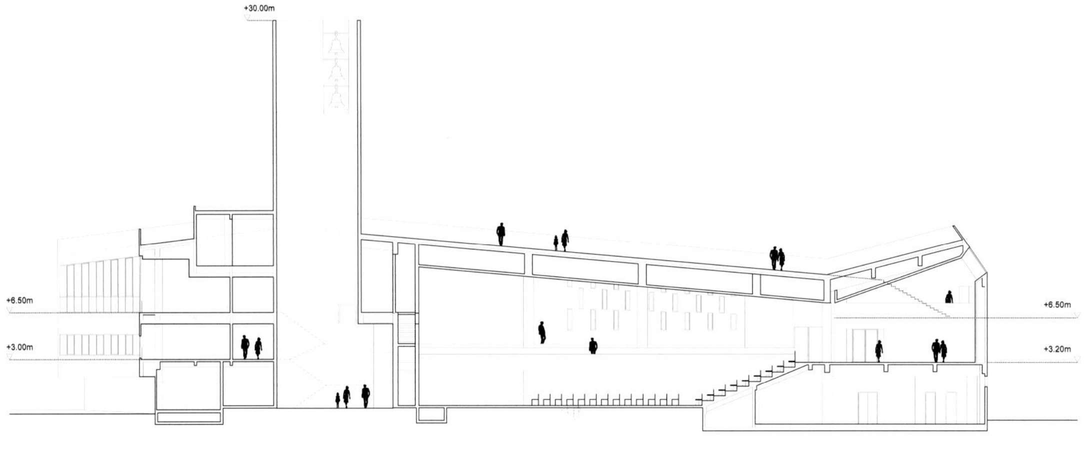

Section B-B

SHOU COUNTY CULTURE AND ART CENTER

Studio Zhu-Pei

Location: Shou County, Anhui Province
Architect: Studio Zhu-Pei
Principal architect: Zhu Pei
Design team: You Changchen, Shuhei Nakamura, Liu Ling, Wu Zhigang, Yang Shengchen, Du Yang, Ke Jun, Ding Xinyue, Wu Zhenhe, Du Yao
Structural and MEP engineer: BIAD JAMA CO., LTD.
Landscape and interior: Studio Zhu-Pei, The Design Institute of Landscape and Architecture China Academy of Art
Area: 30,010 square meters
Project completion: 2019
Photography: Su Shengliang

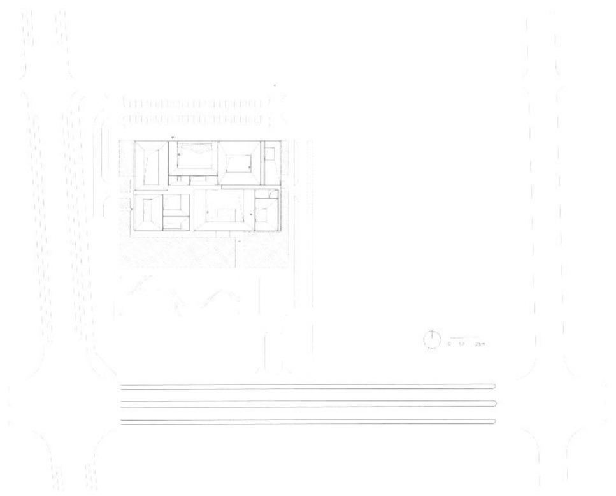

Site plan

Shou County is located in the center of Anhui Province, on the south bank of Huai River. In ancient times, it was the home of the Chu culture and where Liu An, King of Huainan, edited a compendium of ancient Chinese philosophy and composed poetry. The old town of Shou County is roughly square in shape and surrounded by rammed earth walls, with the outward-facing sides of the walls covered in brick above an elevated stone foundation. The entire wall is inclined slightly inwards to allow the stone layers at the bottom to sit firmly in place. The city moat lies to the southeast of the city; Fei River to the north; Shouxi Lake to the west; and Bagong Mountains can be seen in the distance. A walk across the ancient bridges, a stroll through the old town, or an exploration of the ancient relics can offer boundless inspiration. The city walls wrap tightly around

Shou County Culture and Art Center

Main entrance

the chaotic, scattered, and diverse buildings of the city, creating a sudden change in the experience of the environment once the threshold is passed.

The buildings within the city are constructed in the courtyard house typology, which differs from those in northern China and the Huizhou houses in southern Anhui. The typology of the buildings in the old town of Shou County strongly reflects the characteristics of the region's climate, as well as the local culture and way of life. Along the narrow streets, the vertical courtyard houses have small windows and solid walls—a typical weatherproofing feature to protect occupants from the cold in winter and heat in summer.

View to the main courtyard

Visitors enter via a bridge crossing the moat

Shou County Culture and Art Center was built in a new city a few kilometers southeast of the old town, on what used to be empty, flat farmland with a lack of landscape features. Many new tall, generic buildings surround the area and fail to reflect the local climate and local culture. The blandness of the project site resembled a blank piece of paper for Zhu Pei offering the potential for a multitude of creative opportunities. The county government was open-minded in that it didn't insist on specific design requirements, however it demanded the project "be built quickly and completed next year."

The program includes an art gallery, cultural center, library, and archive. Cultural and art centers are not new in China. Many were built between the 1950s and 1970s under the influence of the former Soviet Union. Nowadays, they have been endowed with a range of new possibilities, including creating urban public space for cultural activities. Shou County Culture and Art Center is designed to draw people in to discover and experience it, unlike a beautiful sculpture that can only be viewed but not experienced.

Detail of the Moon Window © Studio Zhu-Pei

Rear garden

View to the rear garden

View from the courtyard to the corridor

The corridor is protected from the rain and sun

Zhu Pei investigated the cultural roots of Shou County, observing old dwellings and ruins, and identifying how ancestors sought balance between the primal force of nature and active construction without modern technologies. The buildings in the old town provided plenty of inspiration. The inward-oriented living patterns of the vertical courtyard houses, and the narrow lanes extending out in all directions connecting houses to one another, reflect the local way of life and hint at the rules of construction for local climate conditions. Zhu Pei reimagined this living and spatial experience to help to embed Shou County Culture and Art Center in the local community.

Multiple courtyards of different sizes are placed in a relatively enclosed rectangular block. They are connected by a winding, undulating public walkway, which is a public loop protected from the sun and rain. The public loop guides people over the bridge, crossing the moat into the building. The extensive front yard at the main entrance forms a public square that represents the *tang wu* (central room) of typical Shou County residences, while the backyard resembles the back garden of local folk houses. Each program of the building has two or three inner courtyards. From the front yard, visitors can wander all the inner courtyards without interrupting the continuity of the rooms. Walking along the protected public loop, visitors can find themselves at times on the first floor, second floor, or third floor. The space is unpredictable, and light and shadow continually shift to surprise visitors, allowing them to feel the artistic spirit of traditional Chinese architecture expressed by the principles of "hide, breath, cultivate, and wander."

The introverted concept of Shou County Culture and Art Center is a sensible choice for the unpredictable future development of the surrounding area. It also reflects the grace, inclusiveness, and vitality of the ancient city of Shou County, which has withstood the test of time.

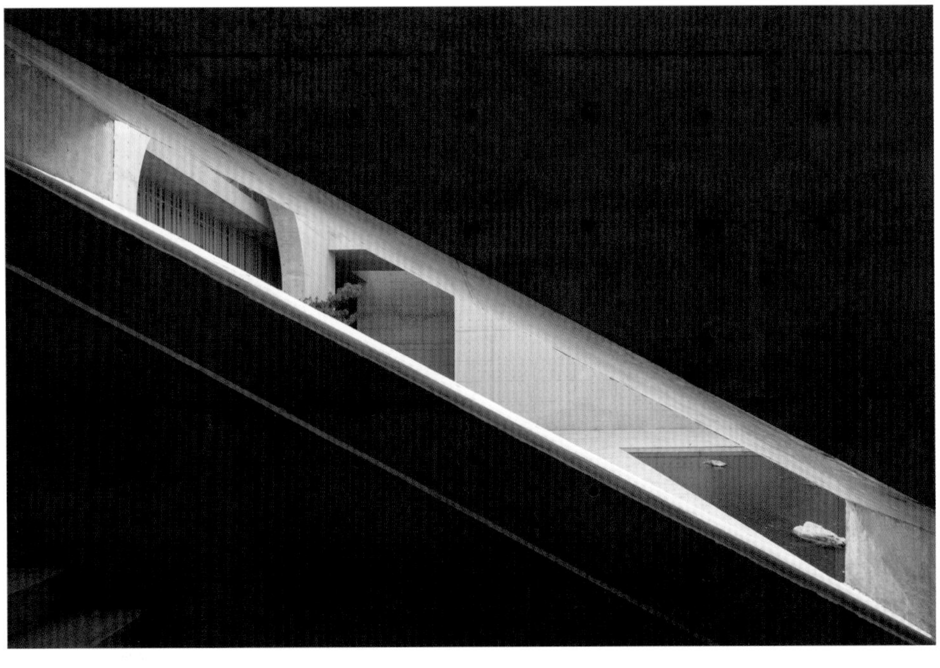

1 1. Textured concrete
2 2. View of a courtyard from the staircase

Inner courtyard of traditional dwelling

Solid façade of traditional dwelling

Interior courtyard of traditional dwelling

Pathways connect courtyard of traditional dwellings

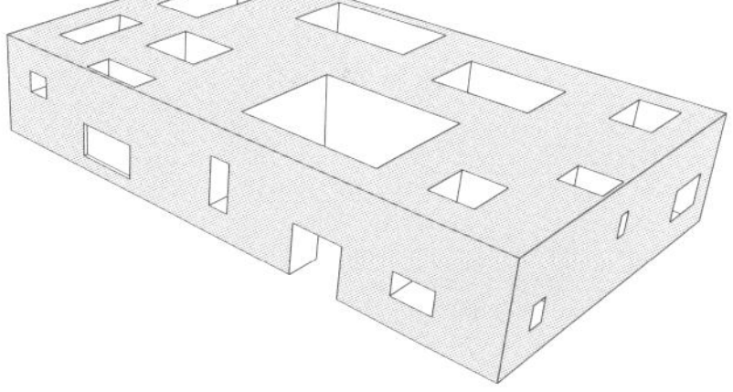

Diagram of solid façade with voids

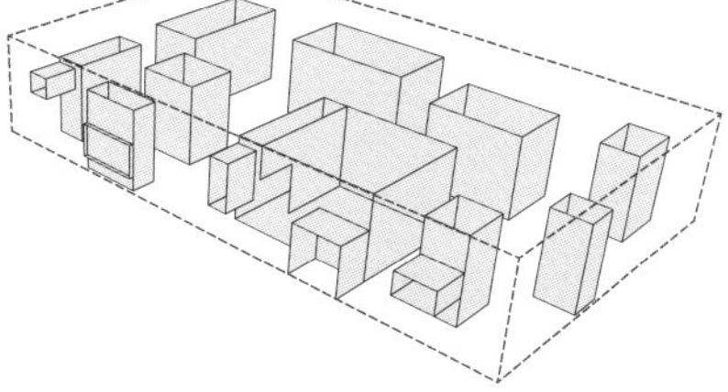

Diagram of inner courtyards

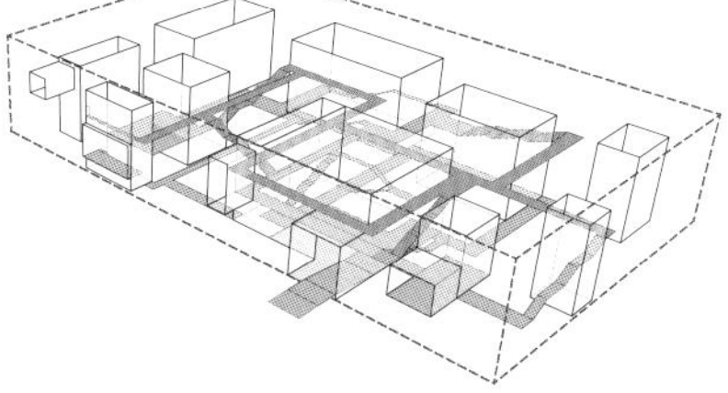

Diagram of pathways connecting courtyards

Architectural model of Shou County Culture and Art Center © Studio Zhu-Pei

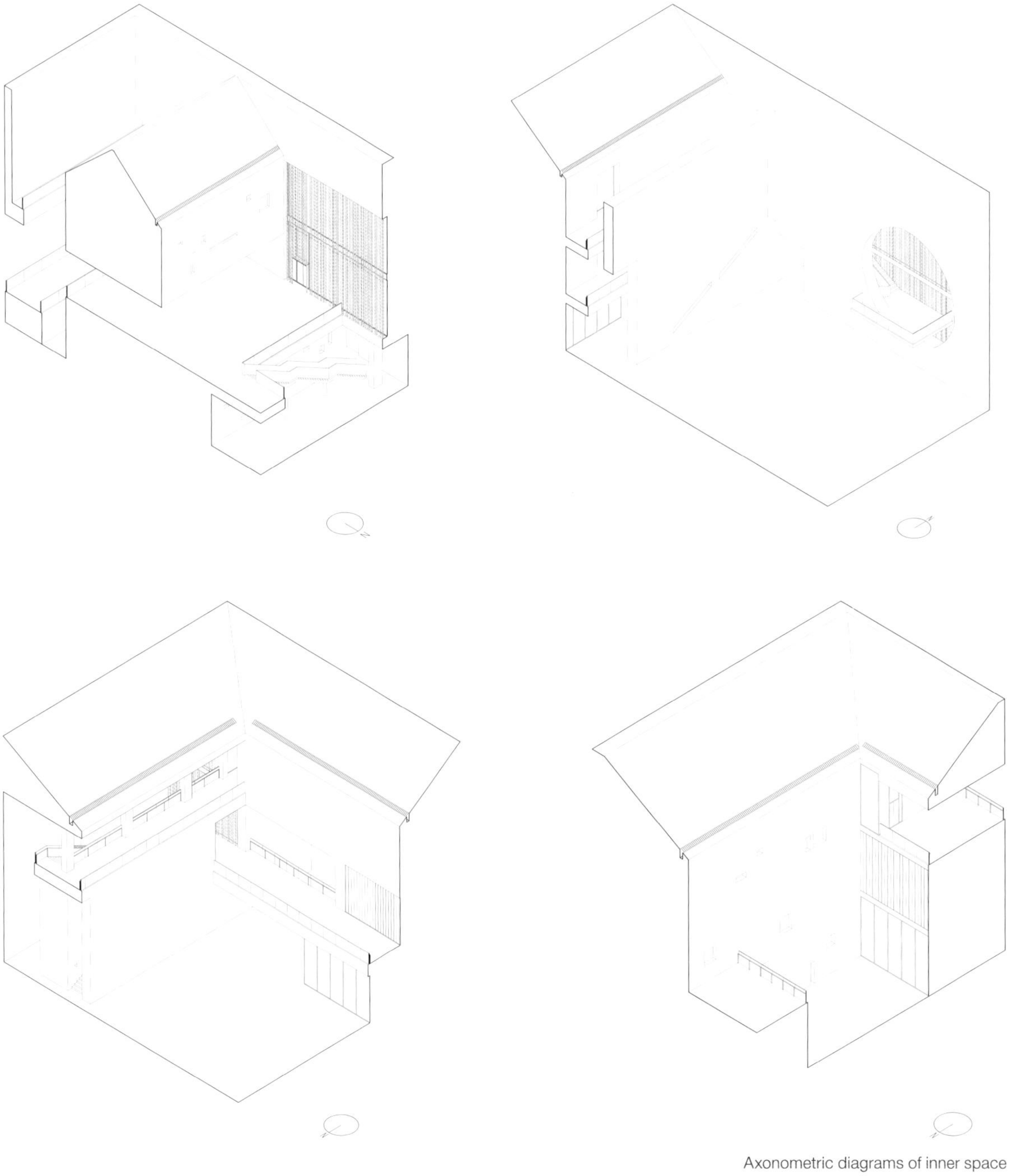

Axonometric diagrams of inner space

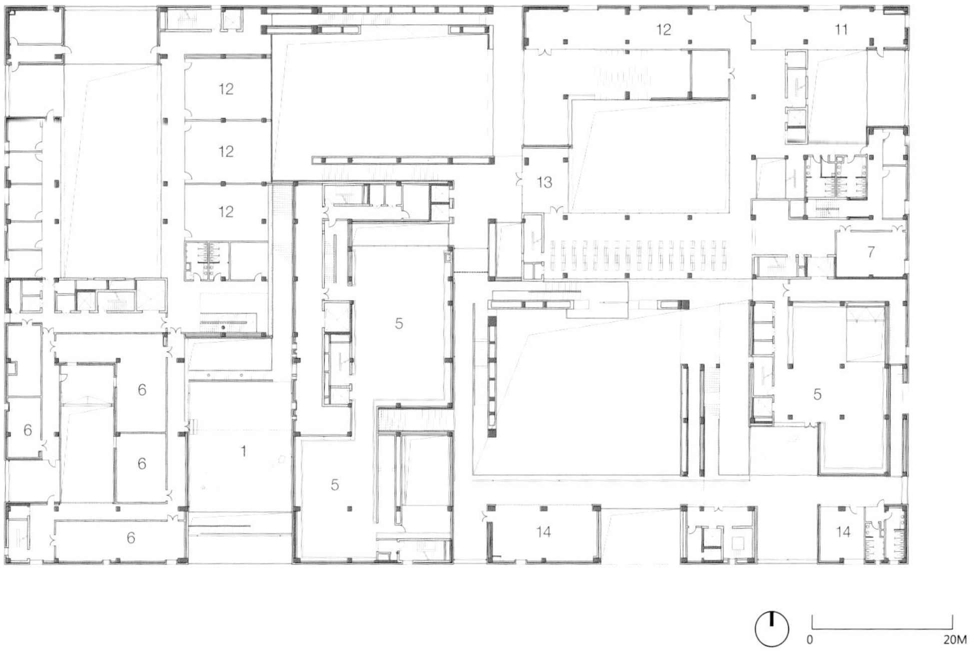

Second-floor plan

1. Courtyard
2. Reception
3. Café
4. Bookshop
5. Exhibition hall
6. Archives
7. Storage room
8. Classroom
9. Lecture room
10. Reading room
11. Multifunction room
12. Multimedia room
13. Activity room
14. Studio

First-floor plan

1. Courtyard
2. Reception
3. Café
4. Bookshop
5. Exhibition hall
6. Archives
7. Storage room
8. Classroom
9. Lecture room
10. Reading room
11. Multifunction room
12. Multimedia room
13. Activity room
14. Studio

Roof plan

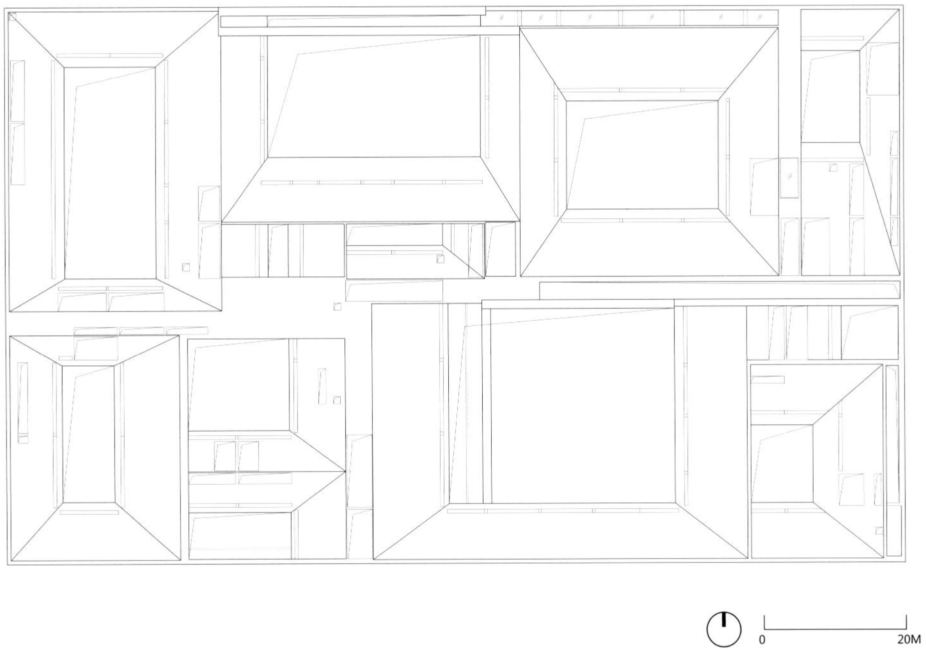

Third-floor plan

1. Courtyard
2. Reception
3. Café
4. Bookshop
5. Exhibition hall
6. Archives
7. Storage room
8. Classroom
9. Lecture room
10. Reading room
11. Multifunction room
12. Multimedia room
13. Activity room
14. Studio

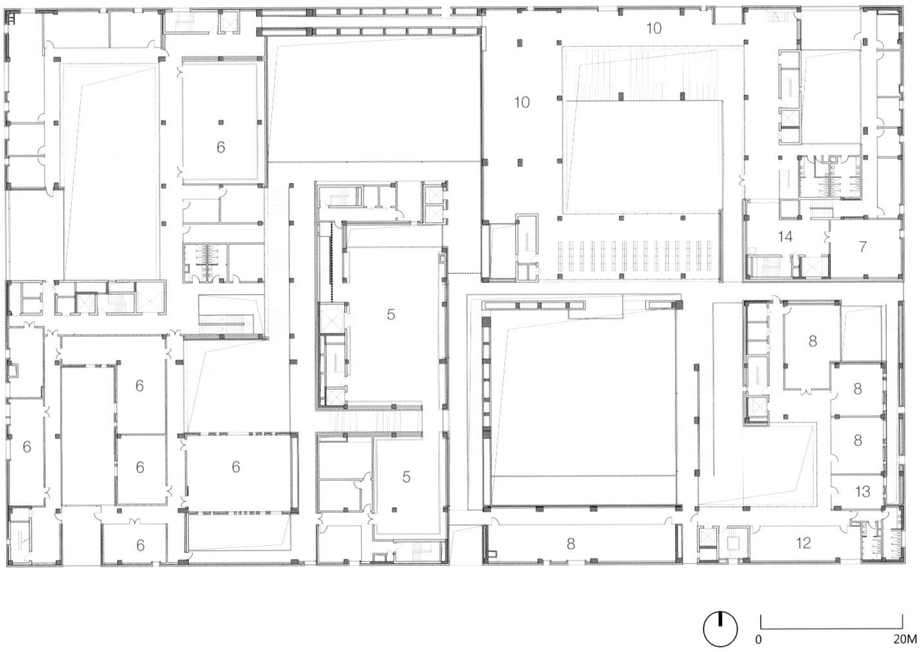

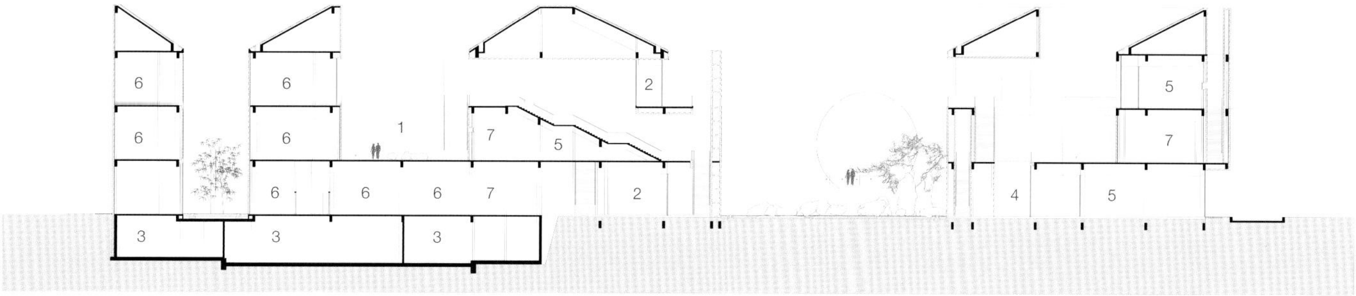

Section A-A

1. Courtyard
2. Reception
3. Equipment room
4. Classroom
5. Exhibition hall
6. Archives
7. Storage

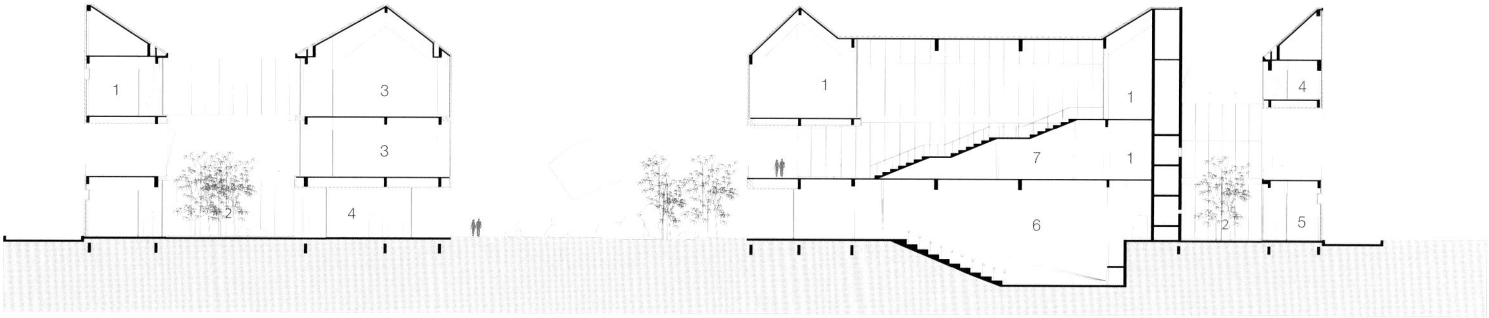

Section B-B

1. Reading room
2. Courtyard
3. Exhibition hall
4. Reception
5. Studio
6. Lecture room
7. Storage

Construction details

1. Roof comprising exposed reinforced concrete panels, concrete fill, extruded polystyrene rigid insulation, polyethylene film, double waterproofing membrane, and reinforced concrete slab
2. Exposed reinforced-concrete hollow structure
3. Façade comprising exposed reinforced concrete, rigid insulation, and aerated concrete blocks
4. Glazed curtain wall with aluminum glazing units
5. Concrete slab paving, mortar layer sandwiching waterproofing membrane, reinforced concrete slab, and rigid insulation
6. Suspended ceiling comprising drywall, flame-retardant panel, aluminum C-profile framing suspended by tie rods
7. Wood paving
8. Fair-faced concrete balustrade panel
9. Tempered glass balustrade panel
10. Floorboards, insulating matting, mortar layer, screed, gravel layer, and earth
11. Rubble layer
12. Paving of gravel

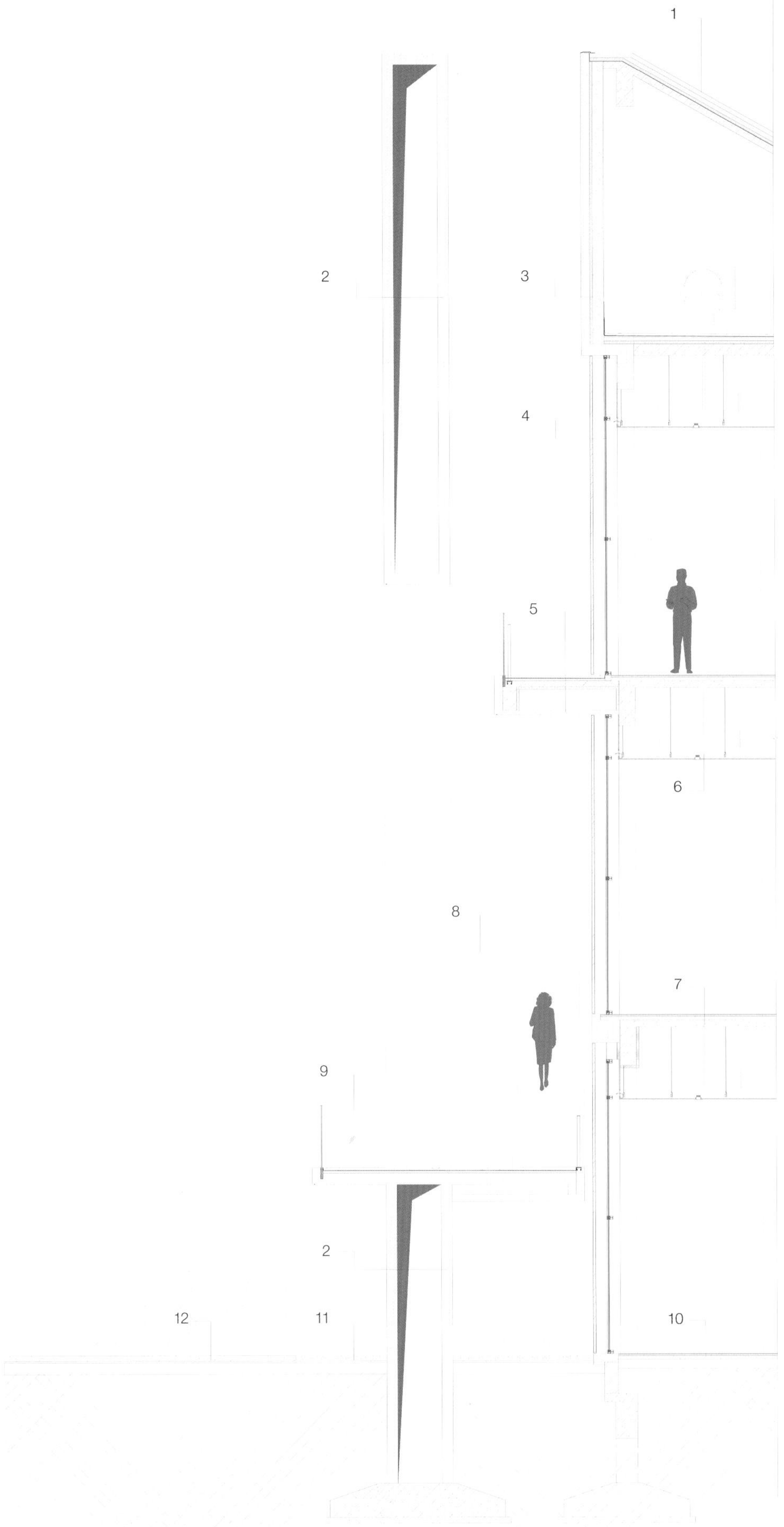

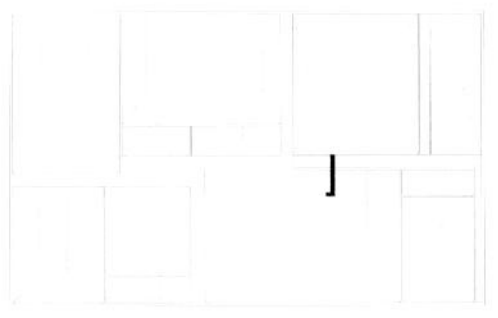

QUZI ACADEMY

Architectural Design and Research Institute of Tongji University

Location: Miluo, Hunan Province
Architect: Architectural Design and Research Institute of Tongji University
Principal architects: Chang Qing, Hua Yun, Liu Wei
Design team: Xiong Bensong, Qiang Jianhe, Wang Ming, Miao Bin, Wu Yuhang, Qi Ying, Zhao Yingqi
Area: 4,355 square meters
Design period: December 2010–December 2012
Project completion: 2018
Photography: Zhang Siye, Zhao Yingqi, Tan Shugang

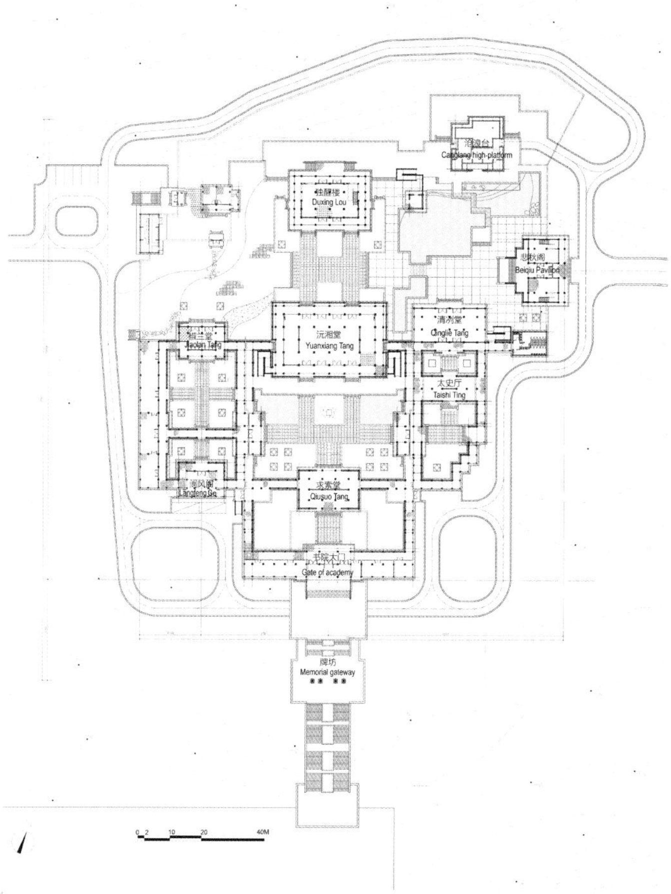

Master plan of Quzi Academy

Qu Yuan (屈原, honorably named Quzi,屈子) was a great Chinese poet who lived during the Warring States period. He is reputed for his contributions to classical poetry and verses, especially through the poems of the *Chu Ci* (楚辞, also known as *The Songs of the South* or *Songs of Chu*). In 2010, the commission of Quzi Academy was given to Professor Chang Qing and his research and design team in Tongji University.

Quzi Academy is the first phase of Qu Yuan Museum in Quzi Cultural Park, which is located on a hill of Yusi Mountain, along the famous Miluo River in Miluo, Hunan Province. It serves mainly to commemorate the great poet and politician Qu Yuan and other famous literary people connected to *Chu Ci* from the Warring States period to the Han dynasty period, including Song Yu (宋玉), Jia Yi (贾谊), Liu Xiang (刘向), Sima Qian (司马迁), Dongfang Shuo (东方朔), Wang Bao (王褒), and Wang Yi (王逸). It also commemorates prominent figures of the later Huxiang (湖湘, another name for Hunan) culture and their associated works.

The academy combines exhibition, commemoration, collection, research, education, forum, and communication in a ceremonial venue and pays tribute to Qu Yuan and other figures. It also hosts seasonal activities, such as poetry recitals during the Dragon Boat Festival, and events that observe the seasonal transition into autumn. The complex has a typical courtyard layout, which consists of three courtyards juxtaposed with each other from east to west.

Aerial rendering of Quzi Academy and Chu Ci Cultural Center

1	2
3	4

1. Handling purlin mortise
2. Making wooden post
3. Installing ties into posts (woven structure)
4. Woven structure in construction

Timber lattice patterns on the window

Detail of brick wall

Danchi (丹墀, holy steps) based on the carving patterns from Qu Yuan age

Danchi in front of the memorial archway

Stone window patterns

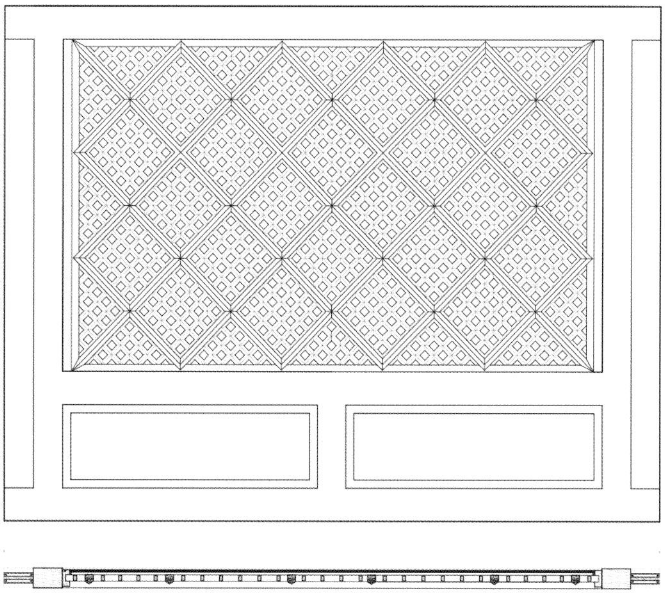

Wooden window patterns

Veiw of Quzi Academy

Quzi Academy has been a famous Hunan academy of classical learning for many centuries. Originally built in the period of Song dynasty(1008–1017), it was once symbiotic with Quzi Temple (屈子祠). Now the existing Quzi Temple is a group of vernacular buildings in the late Qing dynasty style of Hunan, and is protected by the National Relics Preservation Unit. The new Quzi Academy buildings could therefore not be rebuilt on the original site, but on another site more than 600 meters away from the conserved Quzi Temple. This site is on a hill in the south of Yusi Mountain, overlooking the picturesque landscape around Miluo River. Differing from Quzi Temple, the new design abandons simple imitation of the historical style, which only seeks for a fictional representation of archaic styles. The architect discovered archetypal images from the crafted vernacular artifacts, the literature description of Qu Yuan's era, and the Chu traditional patterns revealed during archeological work. The design of Quzi Academy is thus inspired by three sources.

Memorial archway and entrance hall

Gate hall of Quzi Academy

Qiusuo Tang (求索堂) and water courtyard

The first source of inspiration is the vernacular architecture in Hunan Province. This provided the Han (汉), Miao (苗), Tujia (土家), and other ethnic minorities' vernacular courtyard layout, woven wooden structure system (*chuan-dou*), structural elements such as inserted brackets, and decorative elements such as hanging door ornaments, wood carvings, balustrades, and exposed brick walls.

The second source is the architectural and landscape images in Chu Ci. These are the most likely carriers of the ancient style, which offers rich landscapes and decorative motifs. Poetic motifs like the Yuanxiang River (沅湘), Canglang (沧浪), tall parasol trees (苍梧), and Langfeng Mountain (阆风) influenced the design of the scenery at Quzi Academy. In turn, the architecture was inspired by descriptions of *yaosha-hanshi* (实厦-寒室), rooms that are closed during winter and opened up in the summer; terraced buildings on the back of the mountain; multiple deep courtyards; corridors; railings; vermillion wooden wall panels; beams like black jade; square rafters with paintings of dragons and snakes; and the imagery on curtains.

The third source of inspiration is the local archaeological relics with art models and patterns informed by the Warring States period. This includes architectural prototype images that are elegant, simple, and flexible, as well as even-numbered bay layout with the center pillar as the axis, and the decorative motifs and patterns of gods and beasts, panes and *danchi* (丹墀, holy steps).

The most striking feature of the design is the pure wooden *chuan-dou* (穿斗) structure. It has a sloped roof without a curved plane, and even bays with a post in the middle, both of which can be recognized from the three sources of inspiration imaginatively absorbed in the design. One of the deepest impressions from those sources is the building elements divided into two colored systems. A mysterious black is used for supporting elements such as posts, beams, and purlins, and bright red is used for enclosure elements such as doors, windows, panels, and other decorative motifs adopted in the design.

The columns bear the load of the purlins and are connected by tie beams, which are equivalent to a woven frame. Woven frames are common practice in vernacular architecture in South China, and are also known as native frames. The structural integrity perspective of *chuan-dou* is aligned with the saying about Chinese wood-frame buildings: "When the wall collapses but the frame of the house stands." Facing lateral damage caused by earthquakes and windstorms, the structural durability of the *chuan-dou* structure is significantly better than that of the post and lintel structure.

Front of Qiusuo Tang

Yuanxiang Tang (沅湘堂)

Duxing Lou (独醒楼) and Yuanxiang Tang

Rendering of interior of Yuanxiang Tang

Interior of Yuanxiang Tang

In addition to the foundations of Quzi Academy, all the above-ground building is timber structures with mortise and tenon joints. Modern mechanical processing has been combined with traditional construction methods. The wood is the natural anti-corrosion and anti-insect hardwood Bati wood. The length of time the bricks were fired was fine-tuned to form a slight variation in the gray bricks, ensuring the masonry wall has rich distinctions in material and color. An attempt was made to replicate the experience of building with Hunan materials, crafts, and form, and to create a dialogue with traditional artisans and regional craftsmen.

Chu Ci Cultural Center, the second phase of Qu Yuan Museum, is nearing completion. It includes an auditorium in the center and the exhibition, study, and logistics service spaces on each wing. The main part of the building is a reinforced-concrete structure with local stone wall outside. The design is quite different from Quzi Academy, with specific typological transformation through the archetypal analysis. The long thick wall is inspired by the ancient Chu Platform, which is also analogous with the local landform of Yusi Mountain. The steel slope roofs are inspired by the cross ridges roof of vernacular architecture. All of these interpret tradition in a modern way. Chu Ci Cultural Center has layered, overhanging gabled-roof buildings on each wing, which are combined into a whole with the continuous horizontal layer of doors and windows.

1
2
3

1. Corridor outside Langfeng Ge (阆风阁)
2. Corridors and Qiusuo Tang connected between two courtards
3. Beiqiu Ge (悲秋阁)

1. Rendering of Chu Ci Cultural Center
2. Chu Ci Cultural Center

Auditorium of Chu Ci Cultural Center

Interior of auditorium roof

COTTON LAB URBAN LOUNGE

Atelier Archmixing

Location: Changzhou, Jiangsu Province
Architect: Atelier Archmixing
Principal architects: Zhuang Shen, Ren Hao, Tang Yu, Zhu Jie
Design team: Wang Di, Deng Jian, Ye Yang, You Shiyu, Zhang Haochen, Li Jiahong, Xu Ye, Zhou Weinan
Structural engineer: Shanghai Wildness Structural Design Firm
Mechanical and electrical consultant: Jiao Xueyuan, Cao Yang, Lu Renjie, Shen Jian
Area: 6,300 square meters
Design period: January 2017–April 2017
Construction period: April 2017–February 2018
Photography: Su Shengliang, Wu Qingshan

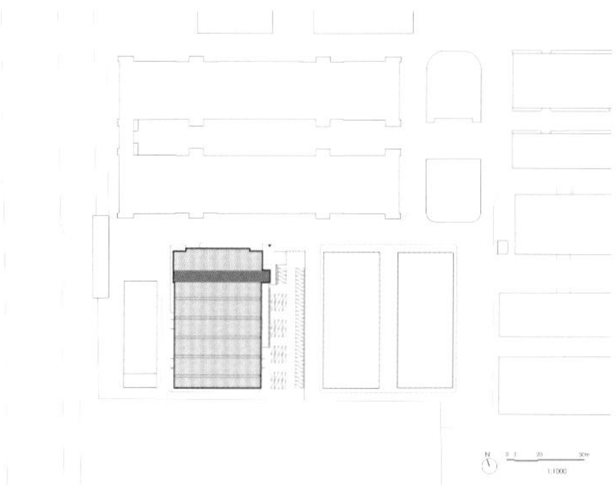

Site plan

Cotton Lab Urban Lounge is located in a former industrial factory, now a technology park in Changzhou, Jiangsu Province. The client had been operating an online clothing store on Tmall and in 2017 they created a store focusing on the aesthetics of clothing and food. They selected a place far away from the downtown area to build a new retail environment for the Cotton Lab brand. In this new commercial model that combines online and offline trading, the virtual store and physical store have emerged as a display "window" and a place for experience and consumption.

Atelier Archmixing faced three challenges. The first was how to coordinate and bridge the gap between the large interior space of a factory and smaller spaces required for retail and catering. The second was how to create an attractive space at lower cost, and the third was how to economically make the new space comfortable, as the original factory building is simply designed and energy intensive." The architecture team undertook a "house-in-house" design strategy, building a new independent structure within the factory building to balance these two major functions.

East façade of Cotton Lab

Lobby

Entrance to Chufan restaurant from the lobby

Main entrance

Transparent chambers within the building

Steel-and-timber chamber of Chufan restaurant

Two high, transparent chambers run parallel to one another in a north-south direction and have the same profile with a steep and symmetrical double-pitched roof. However, they are different in construction. The chamber for clothing is constructed with a white steel structure suitable for the display of clothing. The other chamber has a steel-and-timber structure to provide a comfortable environment for food consumption and events.

The main building is naturally ventilated to reduce heat gain, while the two new structures have mechanical ventilation to provide an independent and fully enclosed air-conditioned environment. This application solves the functional problems and serves as a visual tool to anchor the new structures within the larger space.

The entrance connects with the entries of the chambers. The space around the exterior of the transparent structures provides an area for sports and various other programs aimed at children and adults. These in-between spaces evoke public streets or squares where people can wander during their leisure time.

In-between space within the building

Air ducts and chambers

Entrance to the clothing chamber

Entrance to Chufan restaurant

Parallel chambers

Timber-and-steel chamber for Chufan restaurant

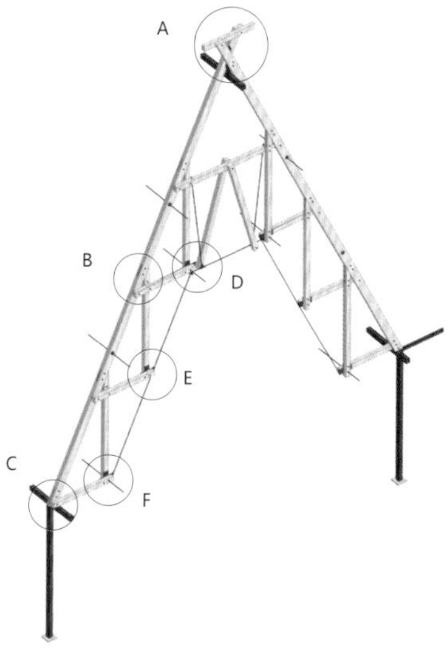

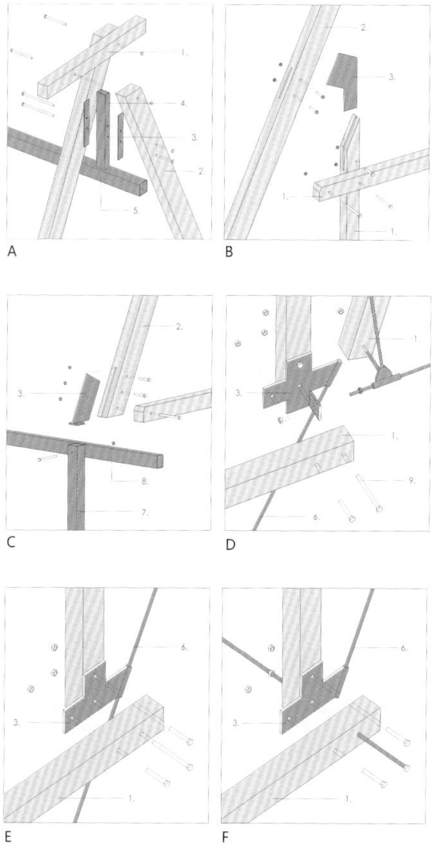

Details of the timber-and-steel structure

1. Timber beam
2. Oblique timber beam
3. Steel joint connector
4. Steel beam
5. Steel beam
6. Steel cable
7. Steel column
8. Steel beam
9. Bolt

Interior of clothing chamber

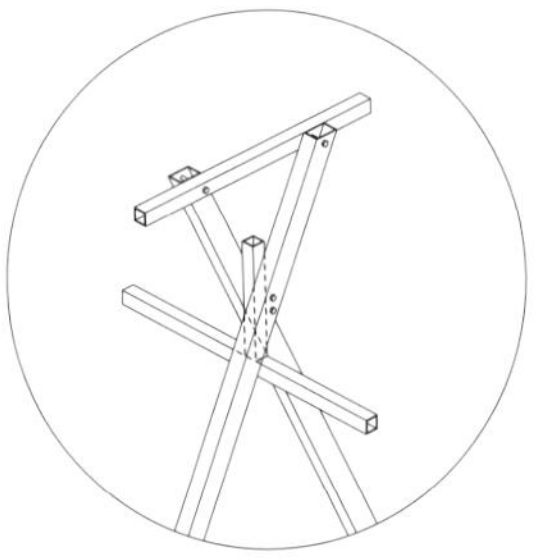

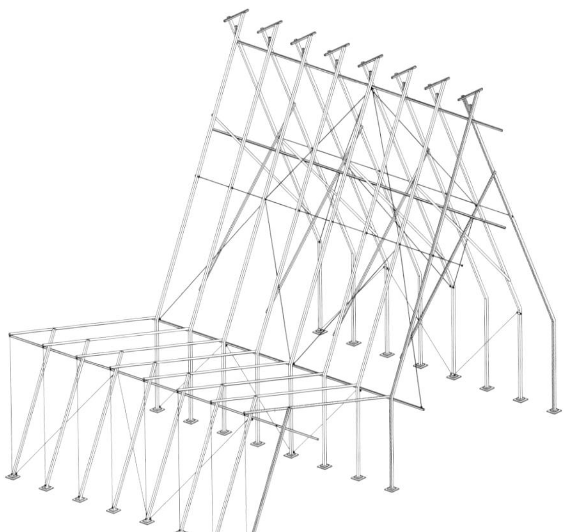

Detail of steel structure

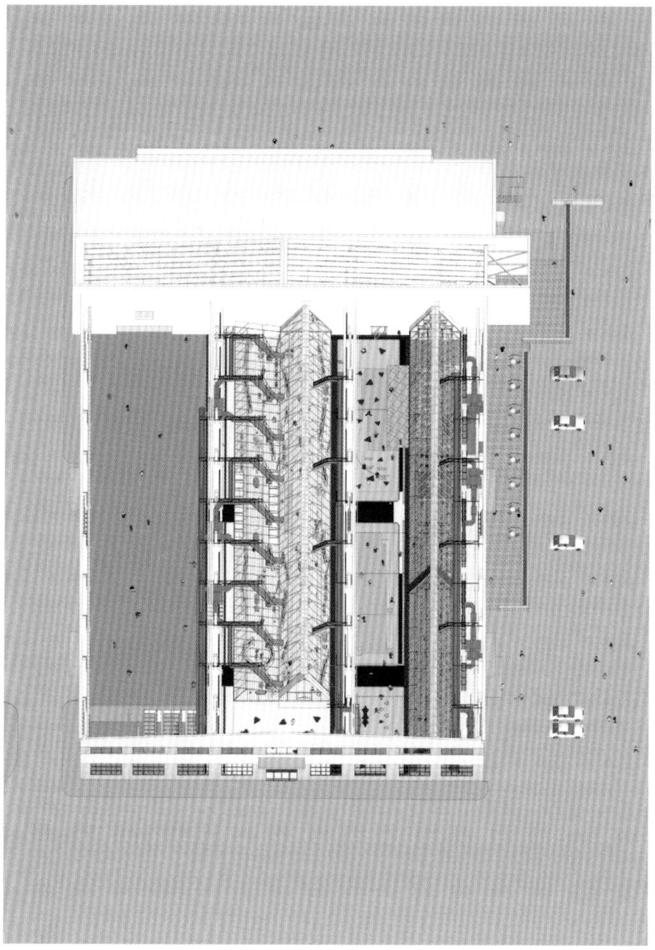

Bird's-eye-view diagram of interior

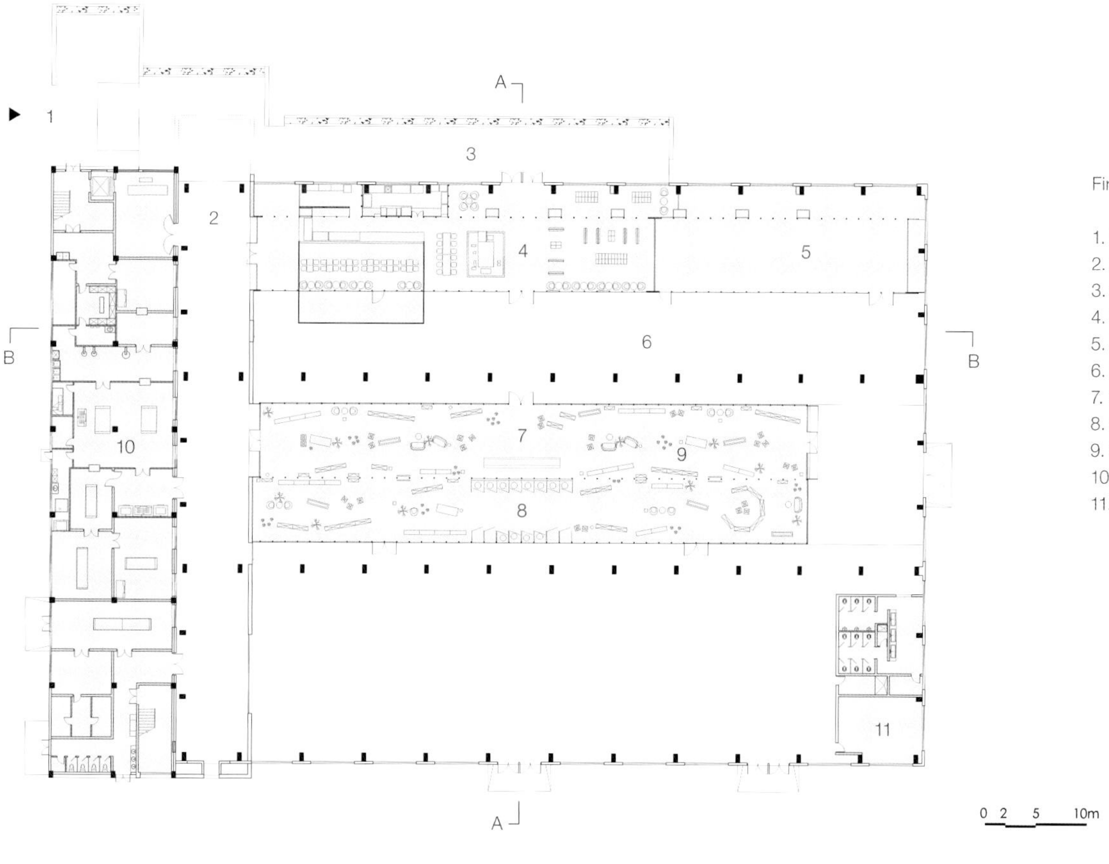

First-floor plan

1. Entrance
2. Lobby
3. Outdoor café
4. Restaurant
5. Lecture space
6. Indoor activity space
7. Counter
8. Fitting room
9. Clothing retail
10. Bakery
11. Device

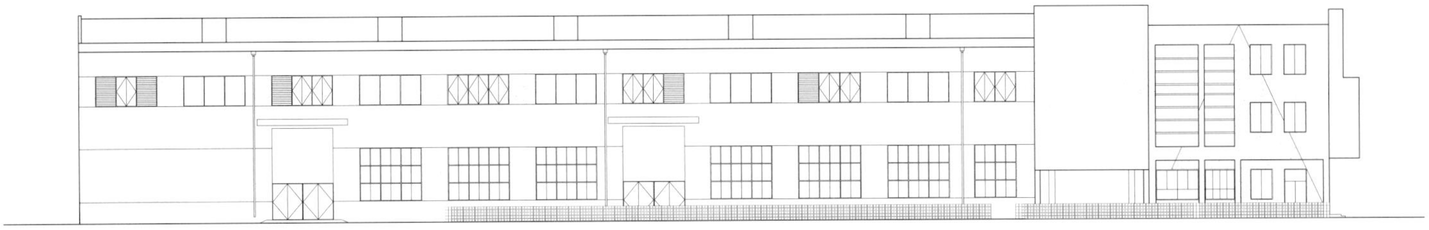

East elevation

0 2 5 10m

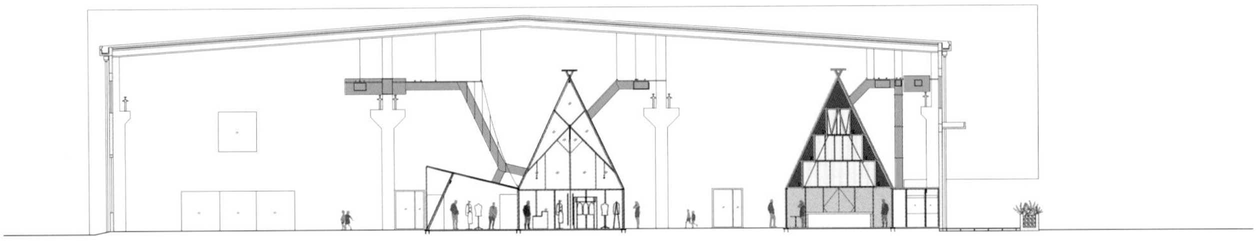

Section A-A

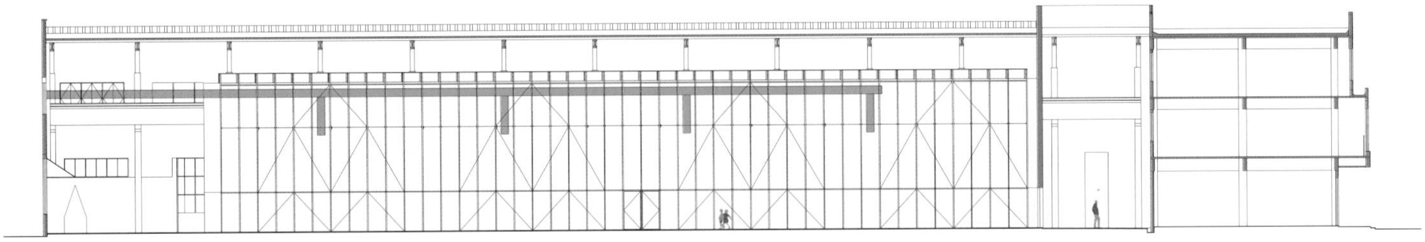

Section B-B

0 2 5 10m

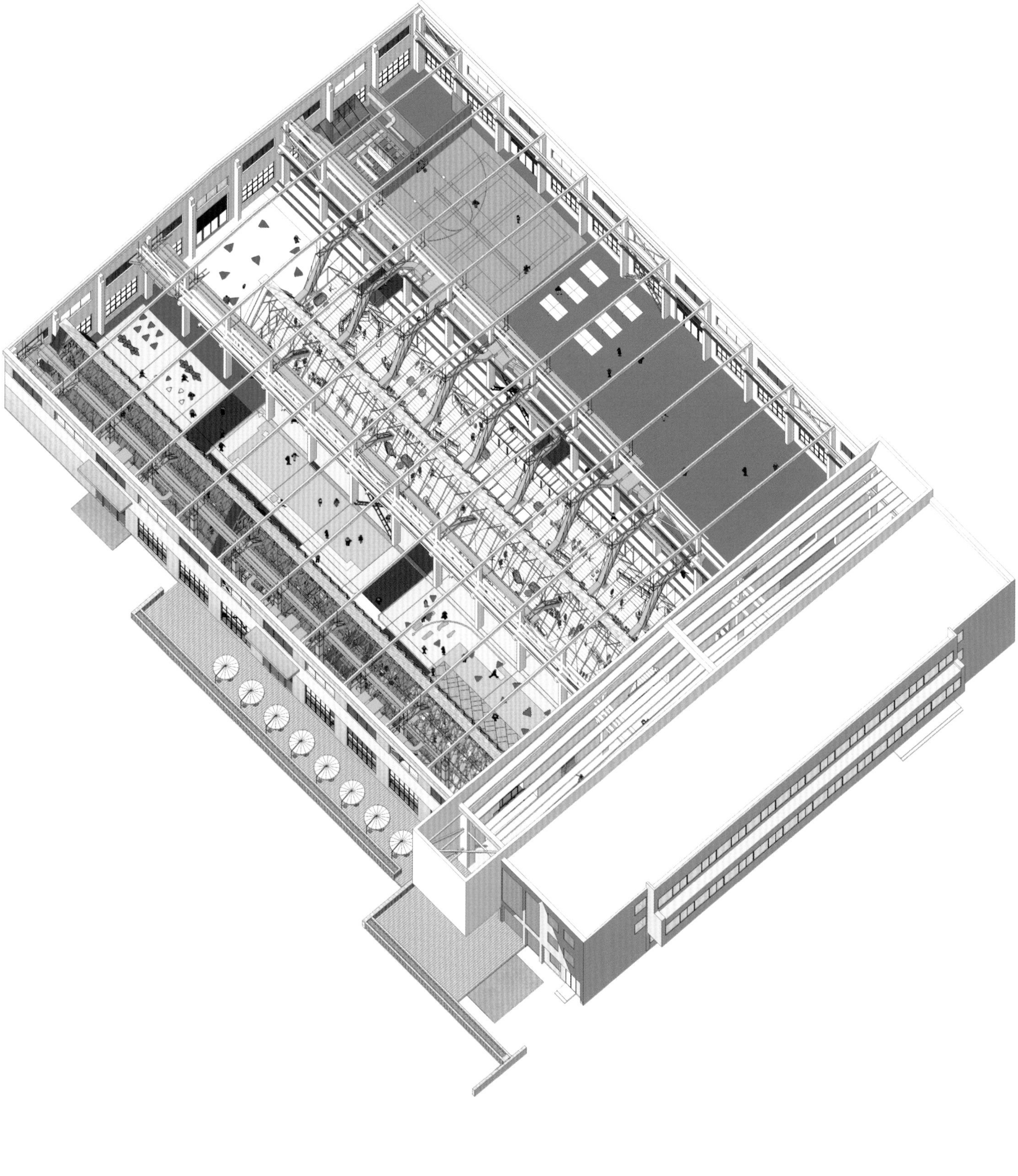

Axonometric drawing

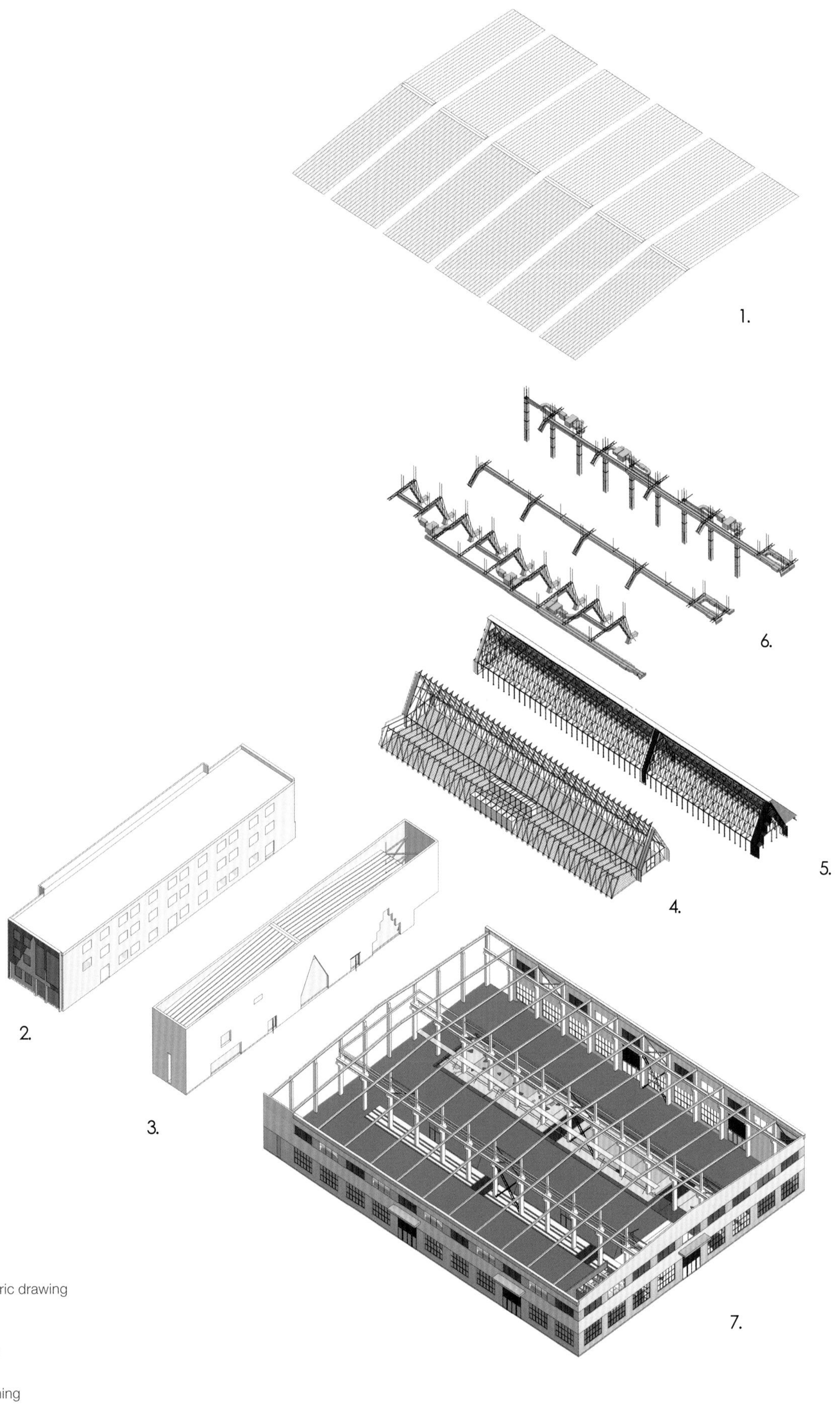

Exploded axonometric drawing

1. Roof
2. Attached building
3. Lobby
4. Chamber for clothing
5. Chamber for Chufan restaurant
6. Air ducts
7. Indoor kids' space

ANNSO HILL HOTEL

Studio Qi

Location: Heshun Town, Tengchong, Yunnan Province
Architect: Studio Qi
Principal architect: Shanshan Qi
Design team: Zhao Yuting, Yang Ping, Liu Nianfei, Ji Guanzhou
Area: 2,500 square meters
Design and construction period: April 2017–March 2019
Photography: Weiqi Jin

Annso Hill Hotel, located in ancient Heshun Town in Yunnan Province, is situated in a narrow alleyway lined with B&Bs and storefronts. The site is composed of two characteristically different lot spaces forming an inverted "L" shape. It begins with a compressed street-front zone on a steep slope, and ends on a long serene hillside lined with beautiful tall trees.

Studio Qi created a layered three-dimensional building in response to the sloping landscape, rather than competing with adjacent shops and façades. The roof gradually ascends 30 meters upward from the frontal tiles that touch the ground on the edge of the alley, allowing for an open public space—a rarity in Heshun. This tilting geometry adds a new complex trajectory that is perpendicular to the linear street, and connects both visually and spatially

Annso Hill Hotel gradually ascends the hill

Hotel overlooking the old town

with the town and the "hidden" hill behind. It brings the backdrop of the forest to the fore, superimposed with the overlapping roofs and walls.

The entrance to the hotel cuts through the roofs and leads to an otherworldly space. Becoming an "architectural field" instead of an "architectural room," it is an ambiguous play between roofs and walls, façades and grounds, elevations and plans. All of the interactive programs and creative activities, such as the café and bar, gallery, DIY, and yoga area, flow against the movements of the transitioning ground. The public space is continuously being redefined by the series of events.

Zigzag entrance into the hotel

Elevated corridor

Staircase ascending toward the hilltop

An elevated corridor connects the guest rooms at the rear of the hotel, set amid the landscape of the serene and tranquil hill. The design of each room is unique in response to the site and exclusive view axis. A 2.5-meter spatial strategy is introduced to identify specific visual movements and programmatic performances within each space. Walls are angled and carved for practical use and to create another spatial dimension. Manipulating the geometric relationship between walls and windows emphasizes the play of light and shadow. All objects in the guest rooms are arranged in the lower horizontal plane, leaving the area above clear for guests to take in the grand views.

Light and shadow across the elevated corridor

Interior of the hotel

Staircases meandering through the interior

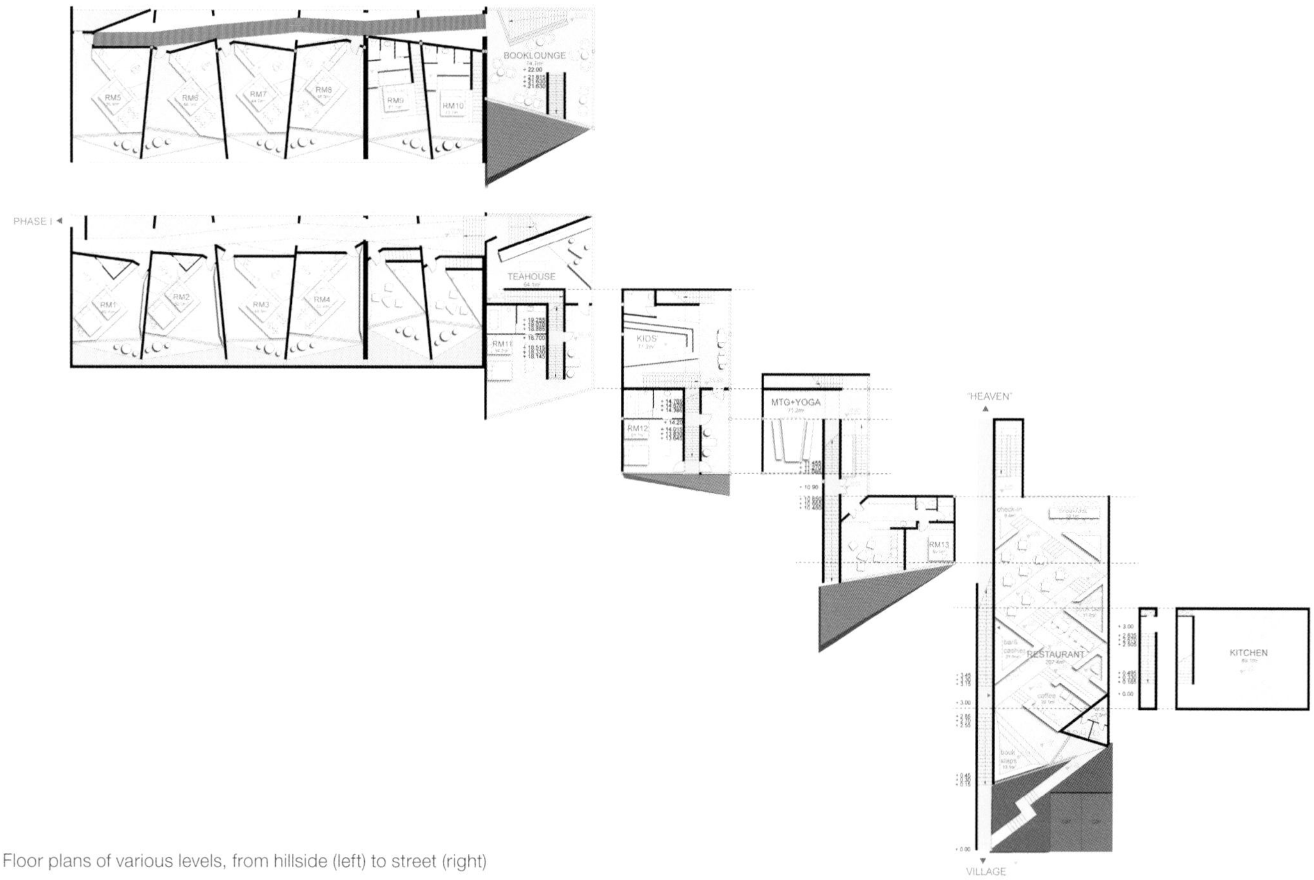

Floor plans of various levels, from hillside (left) to street (right)

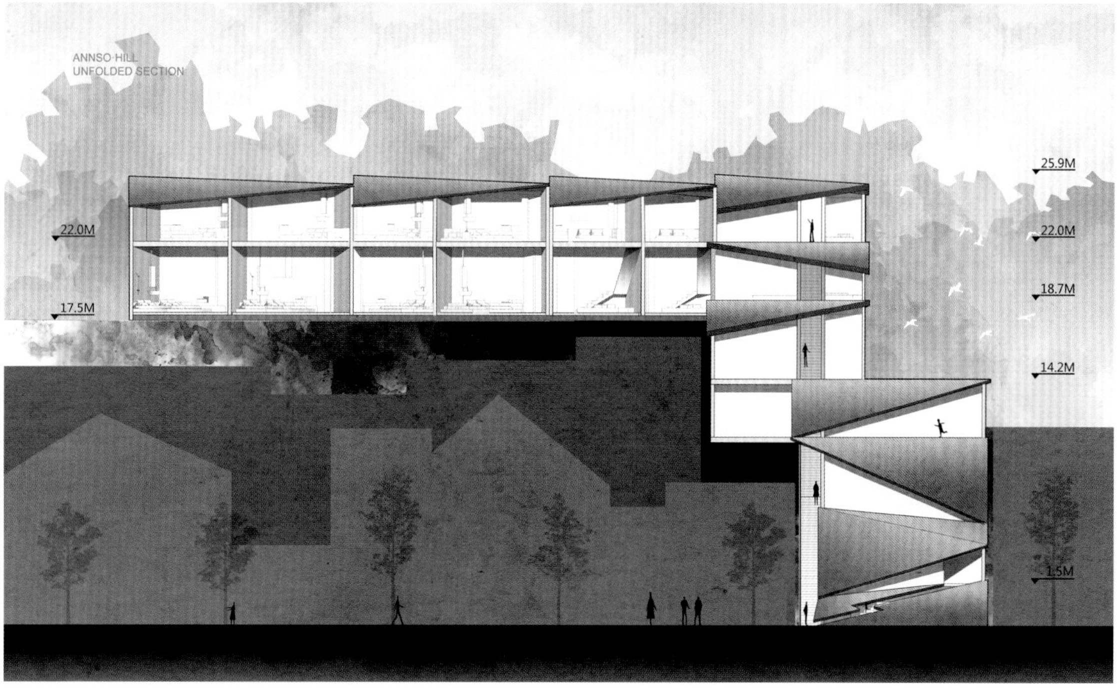

Elevation

Section A-A

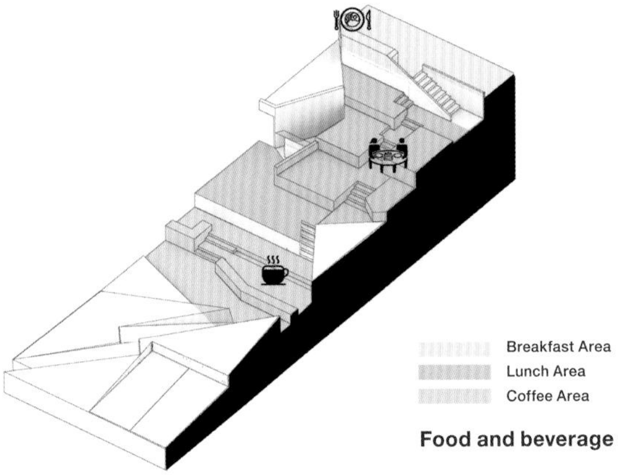

Food and beverage areas

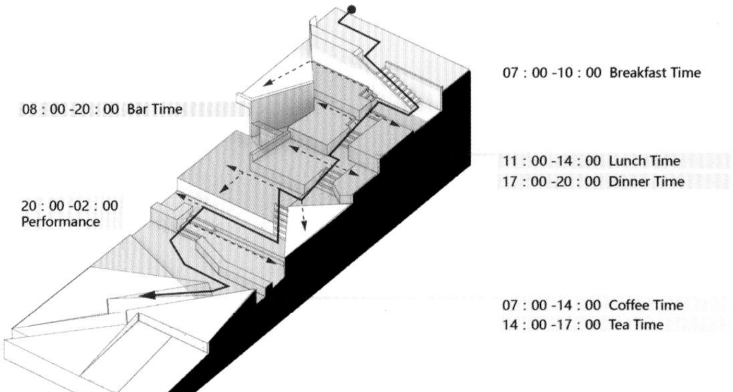

Active time of food and beverage areas

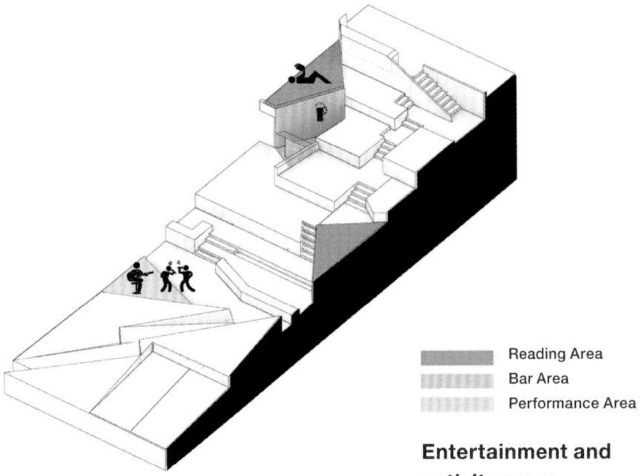

Entertainment and activity areas

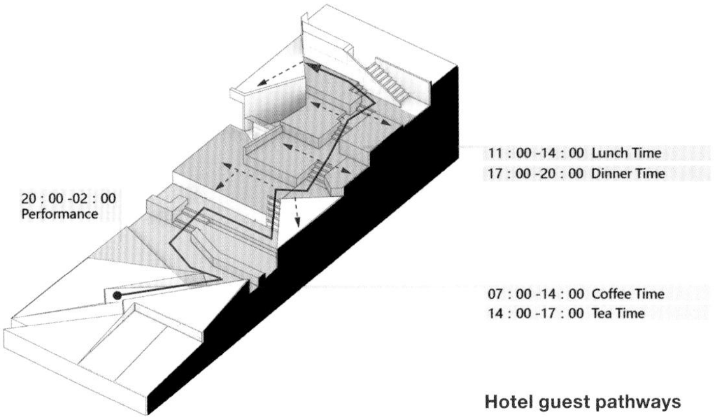

Hotel guest pathways

Analytic diagrams

NEW CAMPUS OF YAN'AN UNIVERSITY

Architectural Design & Research Institute of Tsinghua University

Location: Baota, Yan'an, Shaanxi Province
Architect: Architectural Design & Research Institute of Tsinghua University
Principal architects: Zhuang Weimin, Li Kuang, Tang Hongjun
Design team: Sheng Wenge, Zhang Yi, Xu Tengfei, Chen Rongzi, Ding Hao, Fan Juanjuan, Zeng Linfei, Chang Yunfeng
Area: Site: 60,300 square meters; floor: 74,144 square meters
Design period: 2015–2016
Project completion: 2018
Photography: Yao Li

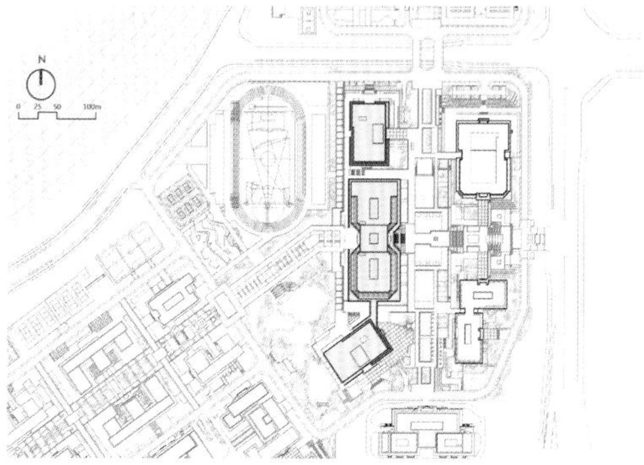

Site plan

Designing the library building—the most important building complex of the new campus for Yan'an University, which has a deep historical and cultural heritage—is no easy task. The design team needed to connect the past with the future; combine regional characteristics with the current zeitgeist; reflect the profound sense of history and glory of the site in a contemporary stylistic language; and express the humanistic desire of staying true to one's mission.

Across China, university campuses are undergoing large-scale expansions, and campus construction inevitably forms a pattern of excessive and convergent styles, thus losing the regional characteristics and sense of belonging. During the initial design stages, the team conceived an ideal appearance of the new Yan'an University campus, and adhered to the concept that character is more important than style. This meant inheriting the spiritual connotations

Exterior of Yan'an University library building

Corner view of the library

and regional cultural characteristics of Yan'an University, rather than seeking out questionable new ideas. It needed to embody the simplicity and sincerity of the Loess Plateau of the northwestern Shaanxi Province and the steadfastness of the historic city of Yan'an.

The architects first researched the spatial characteristics of the site and historical context of the city and university. They studied historic cave dwellings in the region, and reinterpreted regional symbols of the vernacular architecture in a modern vocabulary. They sought out experienced local artisans, selected local building materials, and improved upon construction techniques with the help of modern technologies. They also conducted on-site experiments, comparing the textures and changing colors of the local yellow sandstone, chiseled in different directions and depths throughout the day.

Façade details

Cave-like arcade on the first floor

The Yan'an region hosts distinctive architectural features, and cave clusters with setbacks are extremely common. The design team took inspiration from the step-like cave dwellings to connect the past with the present, strengthen regional elements, and inherit historical context. The cave-like arcade on the first floor borrows from the unique kiln practice of Yan'an. It is made with native yellow sandstone bricks that have been manually chiseled by local craftspeople and placed with a traditional thin joint masonry method. The concave and convex traces on the surface of the stones create order out of disorder, revealing a vivid variety of textures and a monolithic charm. Specially developed split-faced concrete blocks are the main material for the external wall starting from the second floor. The low-cost blocks are environmentally friendly and rich in variation. They embody the heavy yet simple architectural style and demonstrate the original and true aesthetic value of the local buildings. The cross-shaped brick hole is the most common decorative element in the regional architecture of Yan'an. The element is abstractly applied to the parapet wall of the arcade, avoiding the simple repetition of the original symbols. The predominantly khaki color of the campus buildings is inspired by the Loess Plateau. The color highlights the weightiness of the building's atmosphere and becomes a unique symbol of the campus.

The spatial layout of the campus enhances pedestrian convenience, and a series of public squares, courtyards, corridors, and platforms emphasize the role of student activities and interactions as a driving requirement of the space. The arcade is a comfortable semi-outdoor space, providing shading from the sun during summer and protection from snow during winter. It also provides spaces for exchanges between teachers and students and serves as a walking corridor connecting different functional areas on campus.
The cultural tone, architectural style, and environmental landscape of the campus echoes and conforms to the characteristics of the Loess Plateau. This creates a warm, simplistic, and culturally rich campus that builds on the unique character of Yan'an University.

The arcade serves as a walking corridor connecting different areas on campus

Split-faced concrete blocks were specially developed for the building

Interior northern courtyard of the library

Interior southern courtyard of the library

Natural light enters the library from above

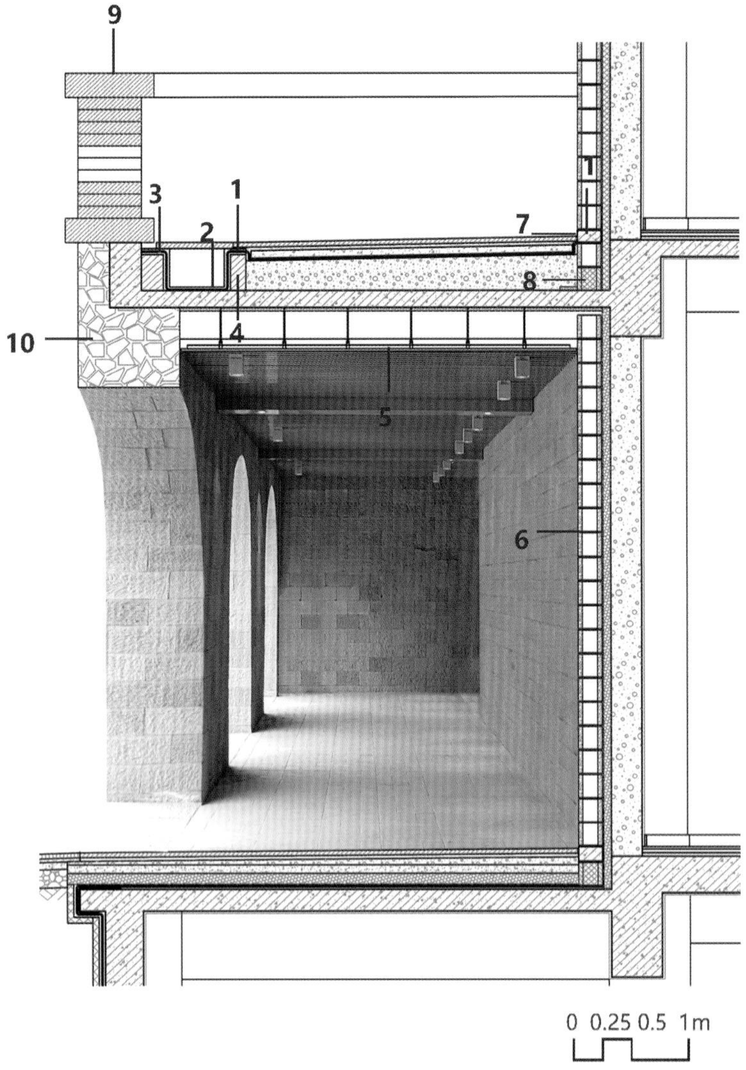

Detail of library corridor

1. Cement layer
2. Granite block
3. Waterproof roll
4. Clay brick
5. Suspended ceiling
6. Concrete cladding
7. Extruded strip
8. Insulation
9. Parapet wall
10. Local yellow sandstone

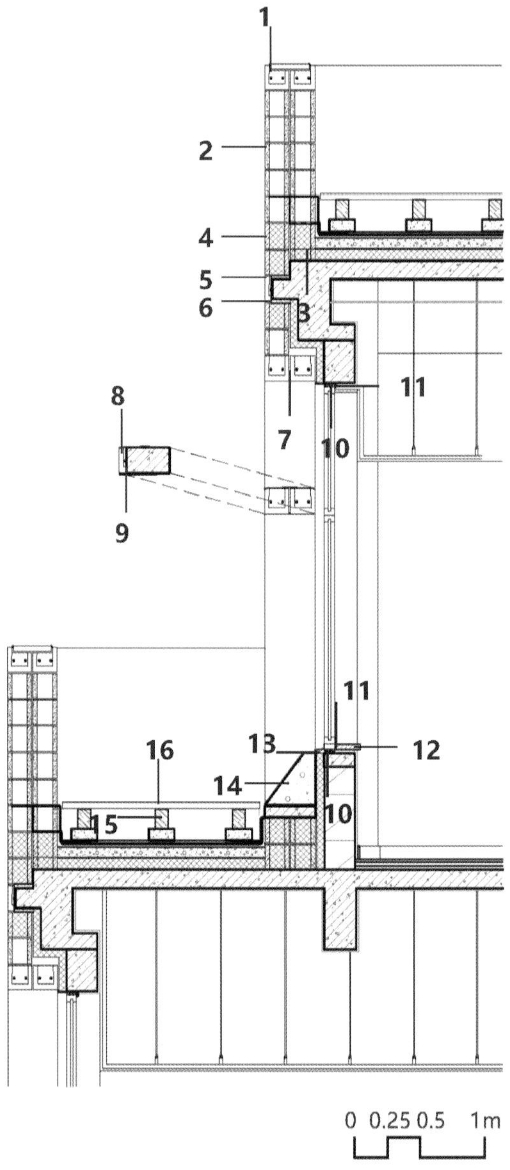

Detail of library wall and platform

1. Filleting of waterproof mortar
2. Concrete cladding
3. Insulation layer
4. Insulation
5. Decorative concrete brick
6. Mortar
7. Pointing
8. Concrete beam
9. L-shaped metal bracket
10. Foam polyurethane
11. Sealant
12. Marble window sill
13. Metal cover flashing
14. Prefabricated concrete block
15. Cement layer
16. Pavement of antiseptic wood

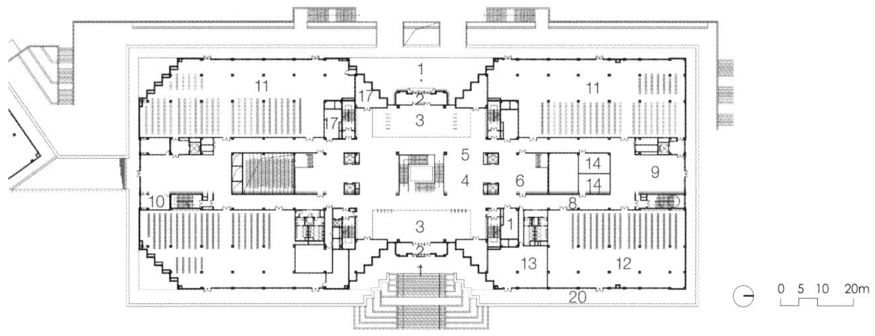

Second-floor plan

1. Main entrance
2. Anteroom
3. Lobby
4. Circulation desk
5. General service hall
6. Promenade zone
7. Auditorium void
8. Corridor
9. Public activity
10. Study room
11. Open-stack reading room
12. Relaxing zone
13. Cataloging room
14. Storage
15. Management office
16. Teachers' activity room
17. Air-conditioning room
18. Duty room
19. Connecting bridge
20. Flat roof of the first floor

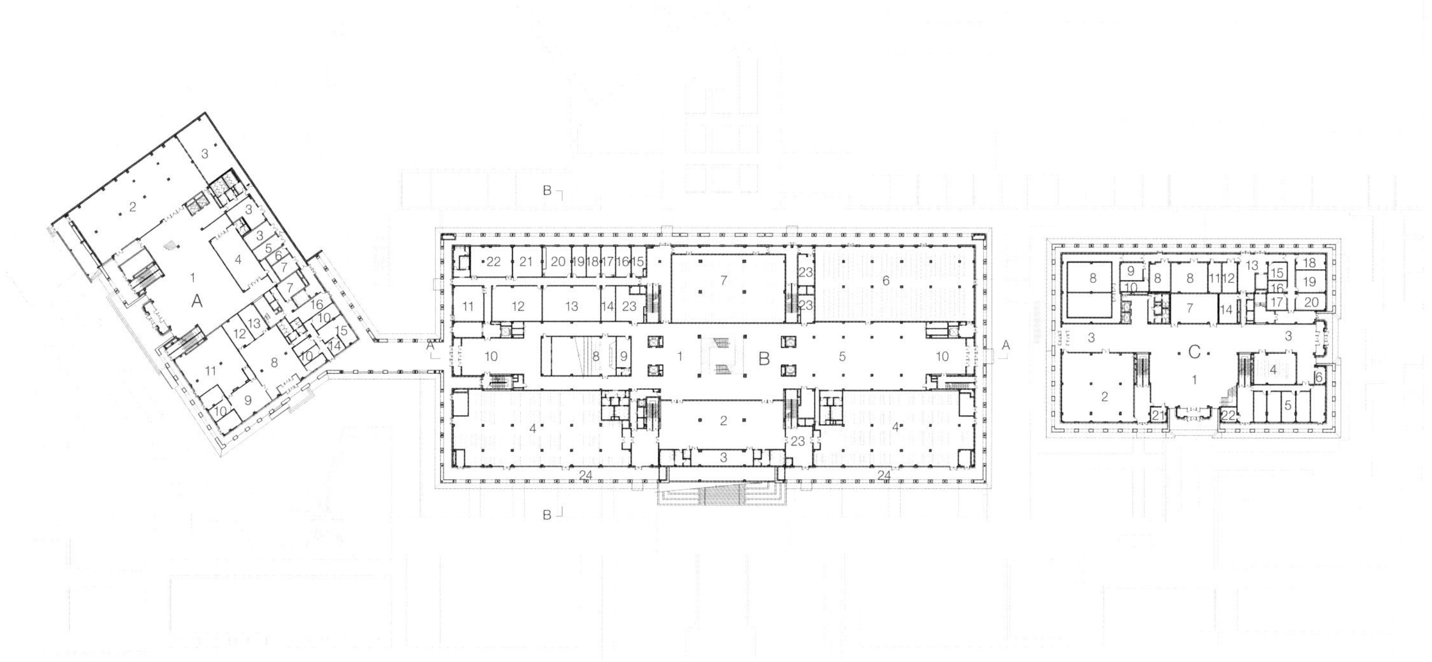

First-floor plan

A: University History Museum

1. Lobby
2. Temporary exhibit
3. Collection room
4. VIP room
5. Temporary storage
6. Document cataloging
7. Air-conditioning room
8. Archives center lobby
9. Reading area
10. Office
11. Archive storage
12. Cataloging room
13. Binding room
14. Inquiry office
15. Storage
16. Small lobby
17. Fire control room

B: Library

1. Shared reading space
2. Café
3. Stationery shop
4. Study room
5. Activity zone
6. Basic stack room
7. Compact stack room
8. Auditorium
9. Lounge
10. Lobby
11. Fire control room
12. Back-issues reading room
13. Cataloging room
14. Temporary storage
15. Unpacking room
16. Bookkeeping department
17. Sterilizing room
18. Xerographic copy room
19. Digital photography room
20. Mounting and restoring
21. Office
22. Network computer room
23. Air-conditioning room
24. Veranda

C: Museum

1. Lobby
2. Temporary exhibit
3. Lounge
4. Multimedia hall
5. Research room
6. Linen room
7. Exhibition hall
8. Collection room
9. Constant temperature and humidity chamber
10. Steel-cylinder room
11. Document cataloging
12. Temporary storage
13. Loading area
14. Air-conditioning room
15. Unpacking room
16. Apparatus room
17. Photography room
18. Sterilizing room
19. Restoring
20. Mounting
21. Fire control room
22. Storage

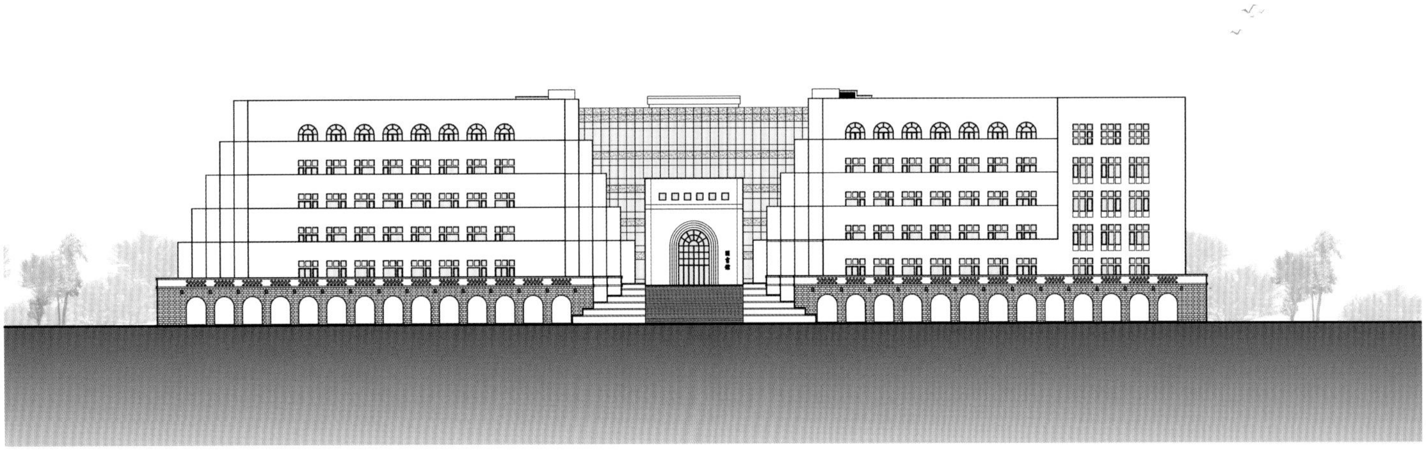

East elevation

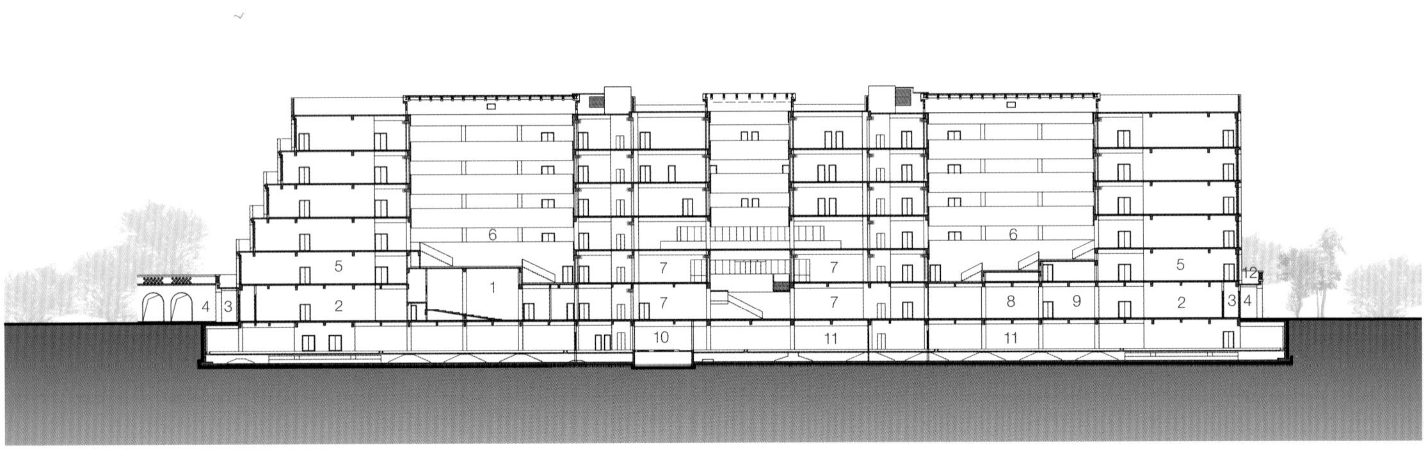

Library section A-A

1. Auditorium
2. Lobby
3. Anteroom
4. Veranda
5. Public activity
6. Corridor
7. Shared reading space
8. New-acquisitions exhibiting space
9. Readers' activity zone
10. Electrical room
11. Underground parking
12. Outdoor space

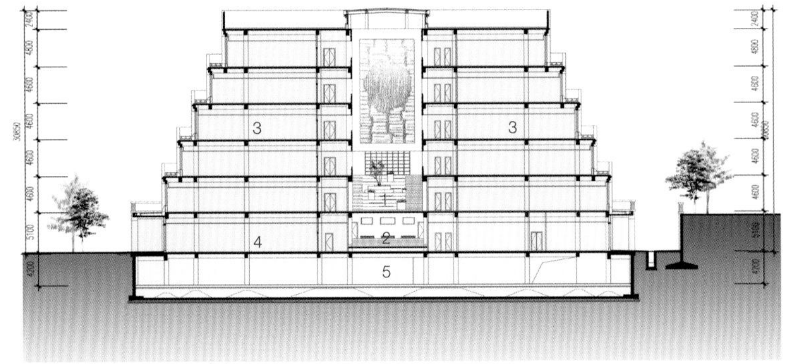

Library section B-B

1. Relaxing zone
2. Auditorium
3. Open-stack reading room
4. Study room
5. Underground parking

FREE BALCONY AN

Drawing Architecture Studio

Location: Daxing District, Beijing
Architect: Drawing Architecture Studio
Principal architect: Li Han
Design team: Hu Yan, Zhang Xintong, Ji Jiawei, Sang Yu, Zhang Yuanbo
Area: 90 square meters
Design period: 2018
Project completion: 2018
Photography: Xia Zhi

Exterior view of Free Balcony An

Drawing Architecture Studio transformed a typical two-bedroom apartment in a commercial housing community in Beijing into a home carrying the spirit of classical space and fulfilling the needs of modern life. At the north end of the apartment a small staggered balcony, given by the developer for free, became the focus of the design and namesake of the project.

Inspired by Japanese architect Terunobu Fujimori, the design team transformed the original balcony into a Japanese-style tearoom. The new curved roof has an attic-like dormer window, and a narrow horizontal window between the roof and breast board of the balcony. The small square window panes create an illusion of scale so that the exterior elevation of the balcony looks like a miniature three-story house.

Attic-like dormer on the curved roof enclosing the balcony

Japanese-style tearoom

Raised floor of tearoom

Drawing Architecture Studio entirely reconceived the interior. The original walls have been removed to create more rooms, giving a rich spatial experience. The division of the space created some small enclosed rooms, such as the study and Japanese tearoom, which are like shrine rooms often seen in a classical space. The floor of the tearoom has been raised and the door beam lowered to create a compression of space. Sitting on the wooden floor and looking up to the curved ceiling, it feels like being in a cave with different shaped windows as the openings of the cave.

Small square window panes of the tearoom and balcony

Living room

Cabinetry, rather than walls, are used to divide the interior space. Cupboards for clothes partition the bedroom from the living room, and storage for books divide the entrance and study. Building cabinetry for walls increases the efficiency of the apartment and creates a thickness for the wall that can only be seen in classical architecture.

There are no strict boundaries between the past and future, the classics and modern, and the local and exotic in architecture. By referring to the classical space and traditional Japanese-style room, the architects explored the form of contemporary living space to create a unique Beijing style for the residential balcony. The architecture team returns to the classics in order to approach the future, and depicts the exotic to develop the local.

A symmetrical plan is used in many parts of the design. The kitchen cabinetry, island bench, dining table, and sideboards form an axis. The main balcony, stool, and balcony doorway are designed as another symmetry. The large window is equally divided by vertical panes that open at each end. The strong symmetrical arrangement added a sense of ritual to the space for daily life.

Adolf Loos' approach to materials inspired the rich palette of oak, painted boards, veneer, marble, red copper, rippled glass, mosaic, and diatom mud. Ceiling materials are extended down some walls, and wall materials are extended across some floors. Thus, classical elements like wainscots and chair rails have appeared.

Bedroom

View from the bedroom to the living room

Interior of Free Balcony An

Cabinetry and sliding doors

Entrance to the dining room

Illustration of the tearoom on a snowy night
© Drawing Architecture Studio

Illustration of the balcony creating an illusion of scale
© Drawing Architecture Studio

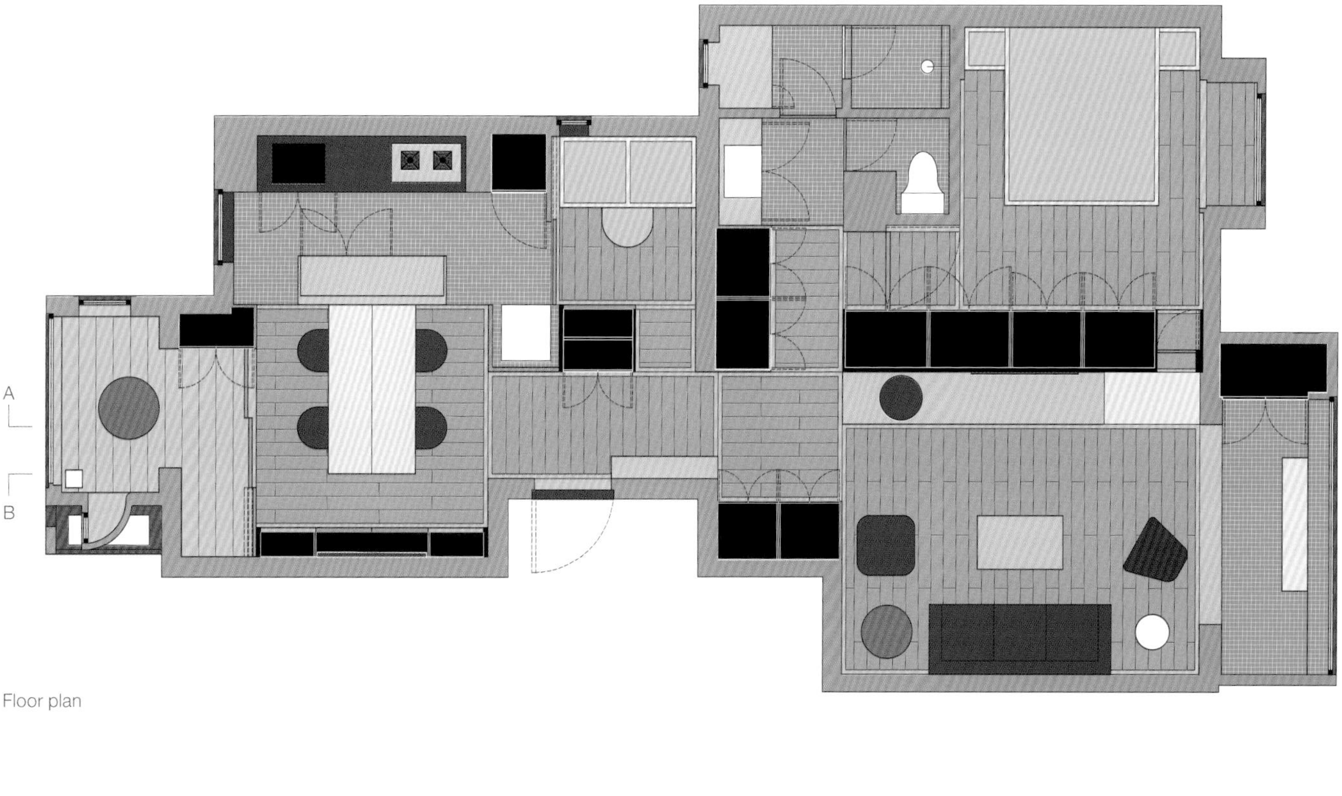

Floor plan

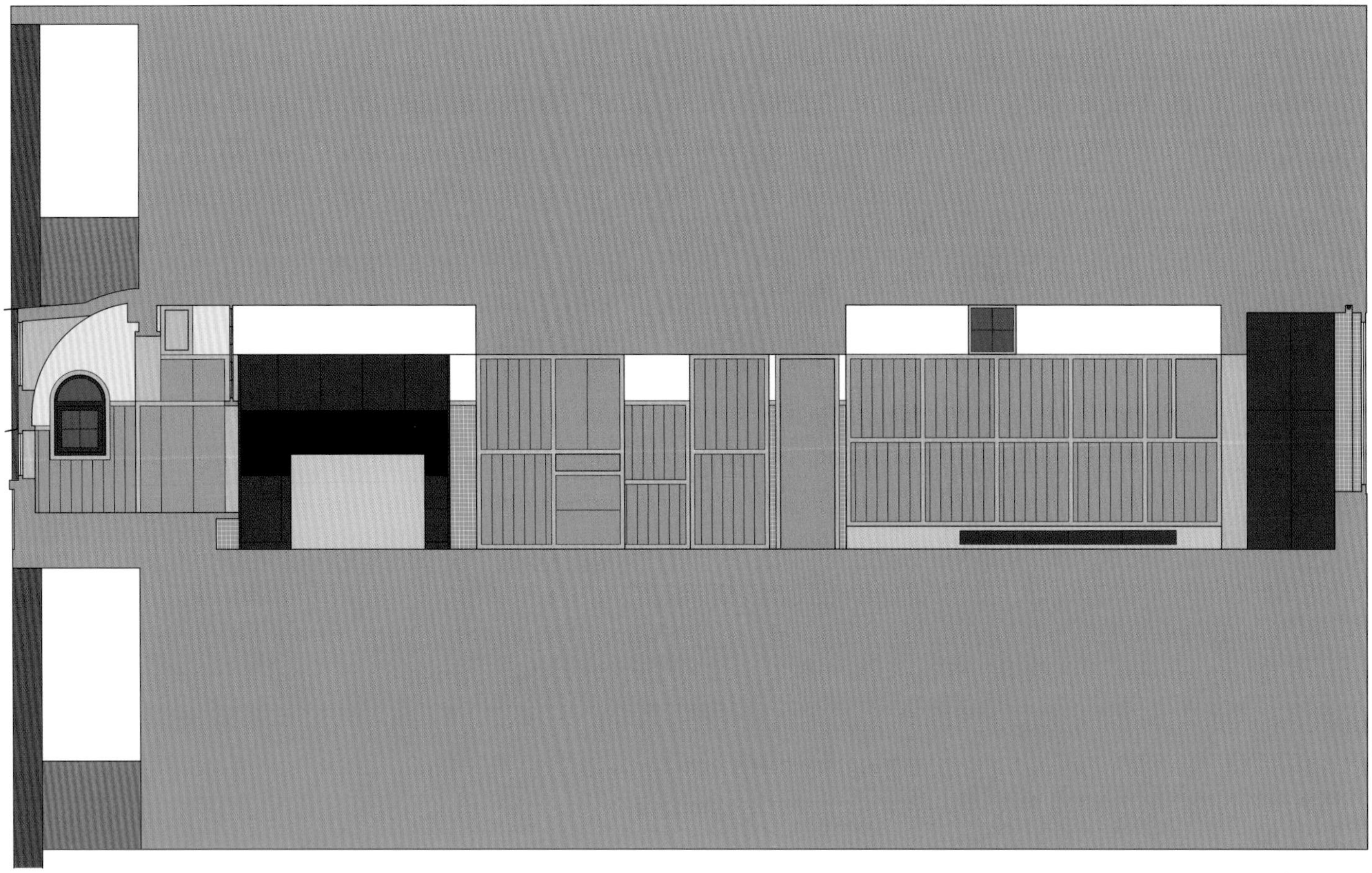

Section A-A

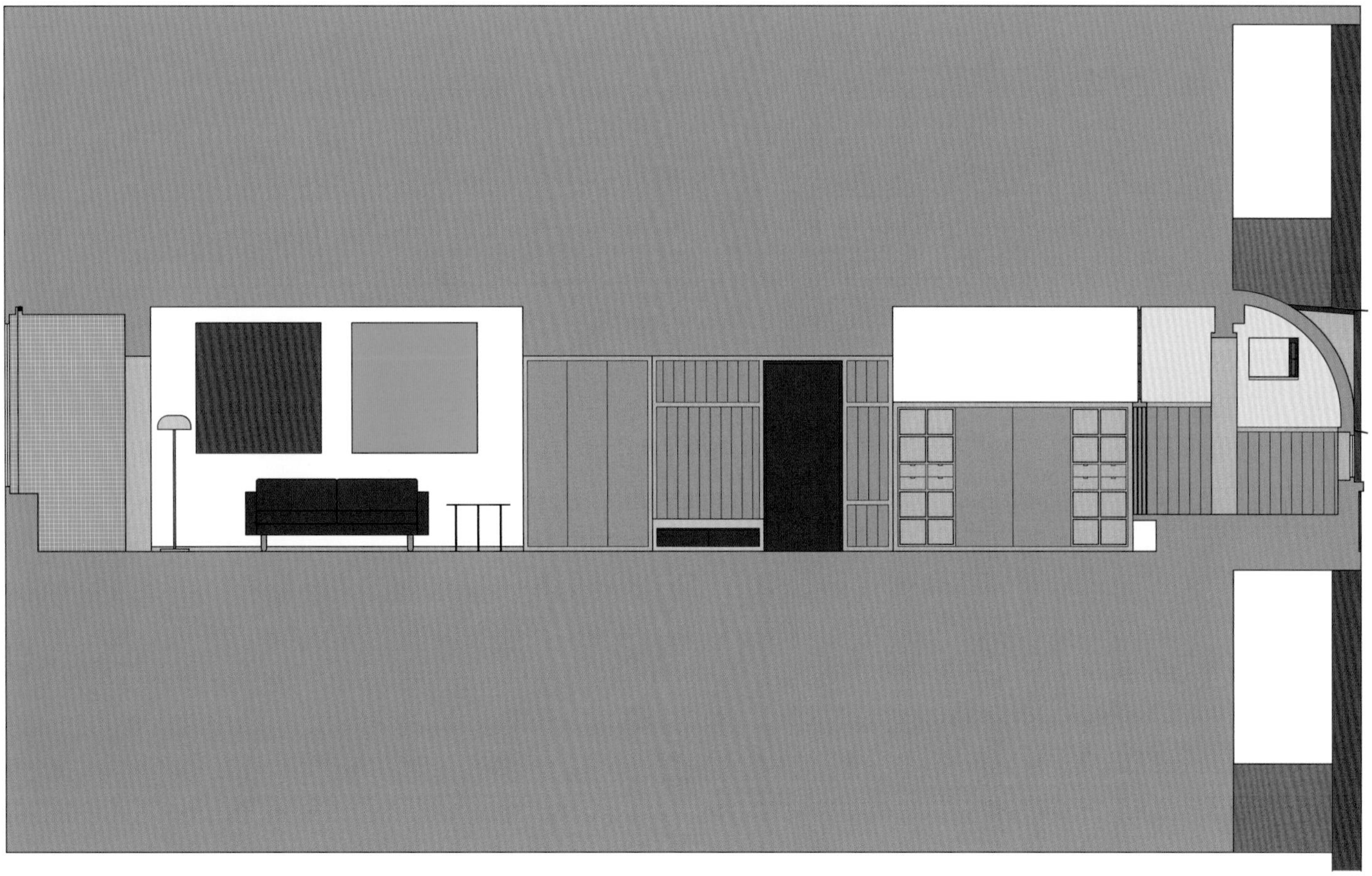

Section B-B

LIGHT OF INTERNET CONFERENCE CENTER

Fab-Union Architectural Technology and Digital Fabrication Co., Ltd

Location: Wuzhen, Zhejiang Province
Architect: Fab-Union Architectural Technology and Digital Fabrication Co., Ltd
Principal architect: Philip F. Yuan
Architects: Xiang Wang, Youyuan Luo, Weizhe Gao, Li Han, Xiangping Kong, Chun Pong So, Xiao Zhang, Gyeongdal Park, Yuying Li, Yating Wang
Interior design: Luwen Liu, Ju Wang, Jingyan Tang, Mengmeng Cui, Yuanyuan Li
Structure design: Tao Huang, Rui Wang
Area: Water Pavilion: 190 square meters; Moon Pavilion: 239 square meters; Red Pavilion: 487 square meters; Cloud Pavilion: 233 square meters
Design period: March 2019–June 2019

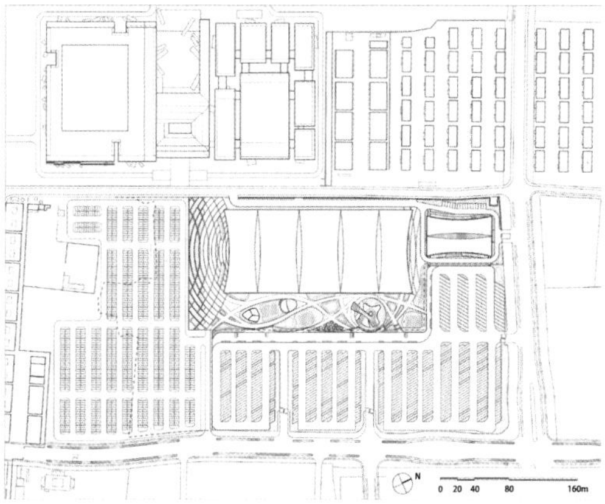

Site plan

Jiangnan, south of the Yangtze River, is a traditional water town. However, internet and digitalization have not only changed the lifestyle of the metropolis, but also redefined Jiangnan. The site for the Light of Internet Conference Center is in the northwest corner of Wuzhen, which is a regular host of the World Internet Conference, also known as Wuzhen Summit. The site is surrounded by farmhouses, tourism projects, and the first stage of the exhibition pavilion area. It is adjacent to the Xizha ancient building complex.

Through the process of urbanization, historical and modern buildings are intertwined, and the use of land resources is relatively loose, showing complex diversity. The layout of the new venues considers the continuity of the space and functions of the existing venues. As the core area of the Wuzhen Summit, it also considers the possibility that the entire area will be occupied by the world's leading internet companies in the future, as well as the development of intelligent and modern conference and exhibition facilities.

The Conference Center pavilion is divided into four exhibition halls from north to south in order to meet the functional requirements of the World Internet Conference and future diversified operation requirements. The interior space can be separated or merged so that it can be used for large exhibitions or to accommodate simultaneous activities. Each section of the exhibition hall is higher in the center and lower along the edge. Beams are placed in the middle of the hall to support the large open space and skylights improve the quality and experience of the exhibition hall. The 20,000-square-meter roof is covered with

Light of Internet Conference Center

Conference Center exhibition pavilion, with public park and four pavilions outside

700,000 tiles. These were prefabricated into 18-tile units that could be quickly installed on the roof.

On the east side of the Conference Center, a public park with four pavilions (Water Pavilion, Moon Pavilion, Red Pavilion, and Cloud Pavilion) integrates architecture and landscape to complete the overall environment. Architecture offers a spatial experience while artistic atmosphere, while the digitalization of design and construction profoundly influences form, material and construction technology, thereby changing the creation and experience of architecture. An experimental building robot was used to build the four exhibition halls, becoming the largest experimental robot project group in the world. Each pavilion is designed for the artistic conception of the environment, and the innovative robotic construction process.

Exterior of the Conference Center

Interior of exhibition hall

Truss structure of exhibition hall

Façade detail

Made with traditional red bricks, the Water Pavilion has interlaced walls with a curved and textured façade that recalls the key element of water in the traditional water town. Performance simulation introduced in the later stages of design development optimized the structural rationality of the walls. A series of rust-steel modular units work in unison with the walls to accommodate various functions, such as the retail kiosk, information center, resting station, and toilets. Fab-Union monitored the quality of mortar application during the entire masonry process and realized an effective closed-loop-construction control. In-situ brick masonry robots prefabricated and hoisted all wall components in just one week.

The form of the Moon Pavilion is generated by three circles in tangent to each other. The double Moon Door is decorated with a display cabinet for conference souvenirs, symbolizing the poetic waxing moon. When the door is open, it offers a welcoming gesture to the broader site. When the door is closed, the seats beneath the eave provide a place for people to rest and stay for a waning moon.

The fabrication and construction process was achieved through digital simulation and robotic timber construction technology for precise processing of all geometric components. Each component was numbered and prefabricated for quick on-site assembly, and designed for demountability and recycling to achieve sustainability. The roof is a radial steel structure, with polycarbonate sheets to allow natural sunlight inside. At night, the artificial light diffuses outward through the polycarbonate roof, casting a crystal clear glare around the pavilion, mimicking the moon on the ground.

The Red Pavilion is the most important focal point of the landscape and inspired by the undulating terrain of the main conference venue. Traditional red bricks are used throughout the pavilion, which follows the brick tradition in Wuzhen but also differentiates it from the surrounding blue-brick buildings. The rainbow form, generated through parametric tools, matches the wavy roof form of the main venue, and references the conference theme of digital interconnection. The form of the structure was optimized through advanced digital algorithm design to generate an ultra-thin structure under pure compression. To increase the speed of construction and reduce the amount of wasted material, the complex structural geometry was broken down into structural scaffolds units that could be prefabricated using robotic 3D printing and bent in place on site. Recyclable modified plastic is used for 3D printing to maximize the sustainable use of building materials.

The Cloud Pavilion is also made out of 3D-printed plastic components. It is divided into three internal spatial volumes, including an indoor café and two semi-open platforms, forming three separate but connected umbrella structures. Four robots prefabricated the pavilion in two weeks. It combines structural performance analysis technology with printing optimization, combining prefabricated production and on-site assembly to experiment with a material-based "digital twinning" intelligent construction method.

Exterior of Water Pavilion

Interior of Moon Pavilion

Cloud Pavilion

Aerial view of Red Pavilion

Exterior of Red Pavilion

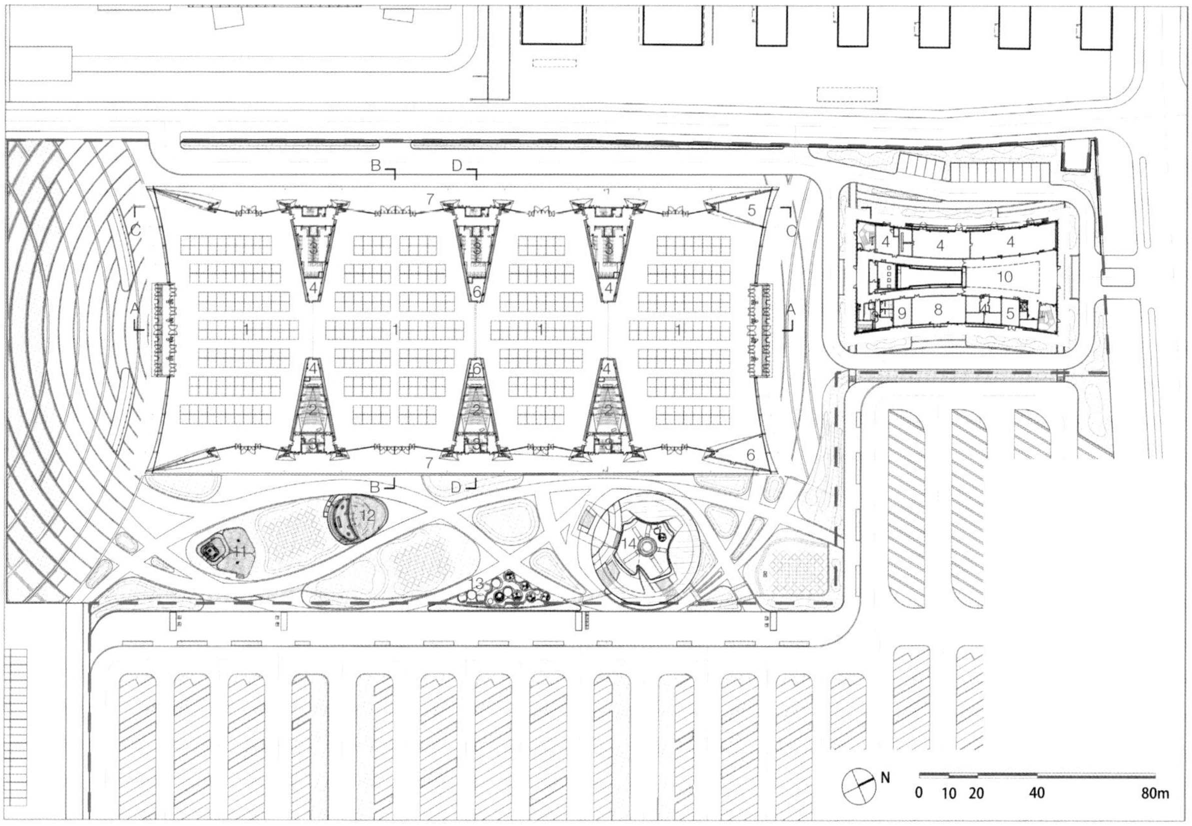

First-floor plan

1. Exhibition hall
2. Multipurpose hall
3. Restroom
4. Equipment room
5. Fire control room
6. Service room
7. Semi-outdoor corridor
8. Cafeteria
9. Kitchen
10. Inner courtyard
11. Cloud Pavilion
12. Moon Pavilion
13. Water Pavilion
14. Red Pavilion

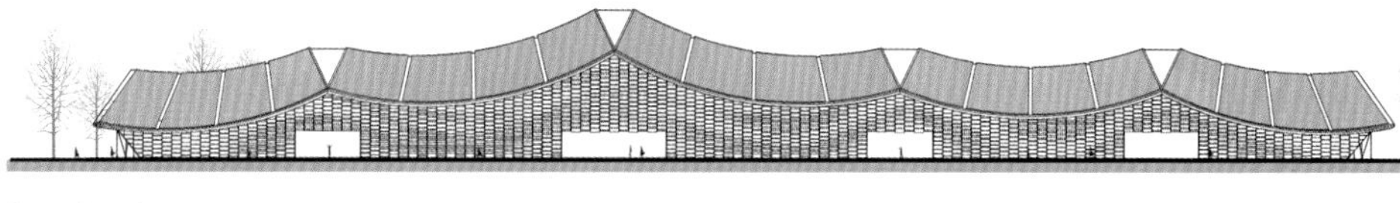
East elevation

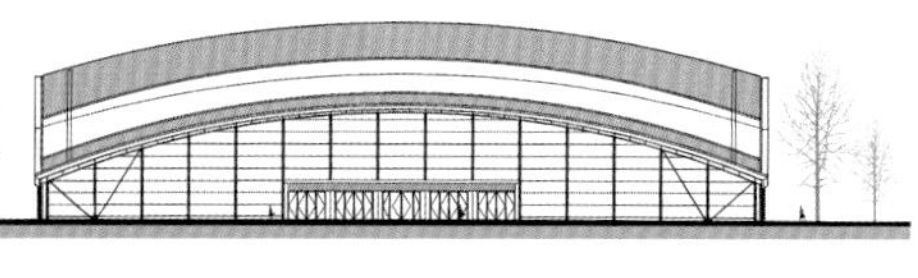
South elevation

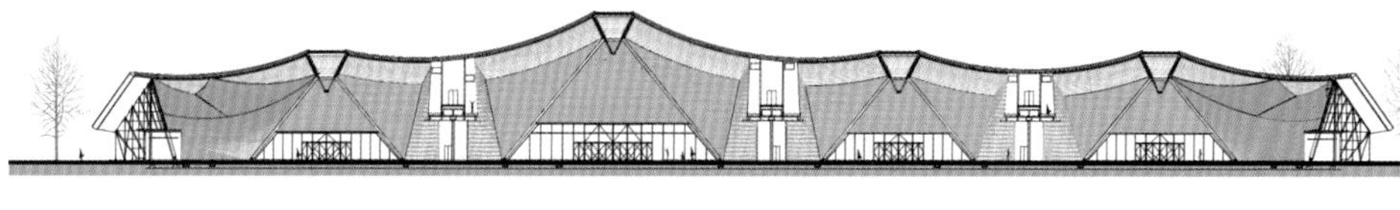
Section A-A

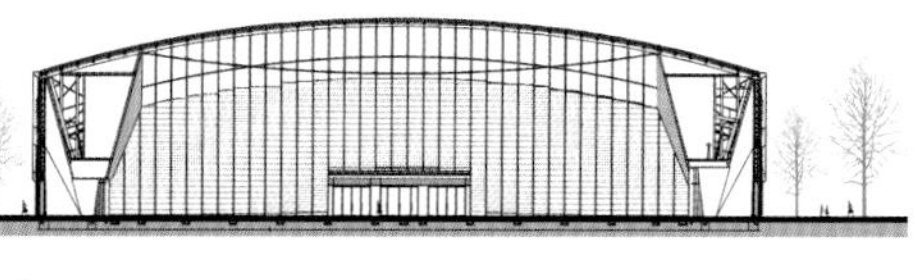
Section B-B

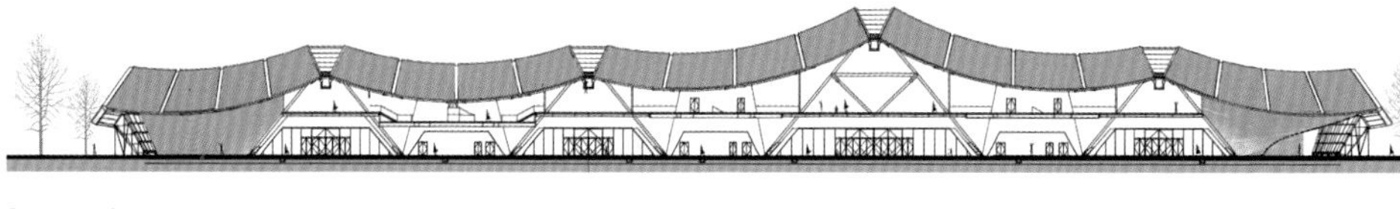
Section C-C

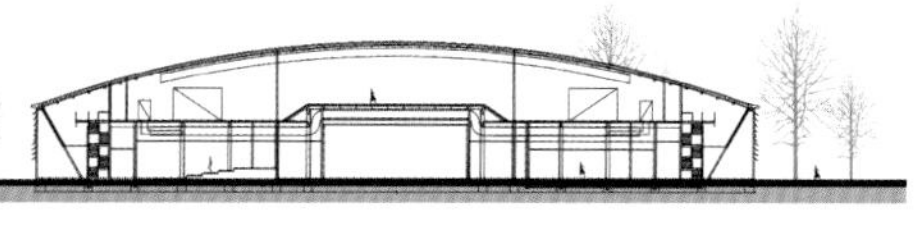
Section D-D

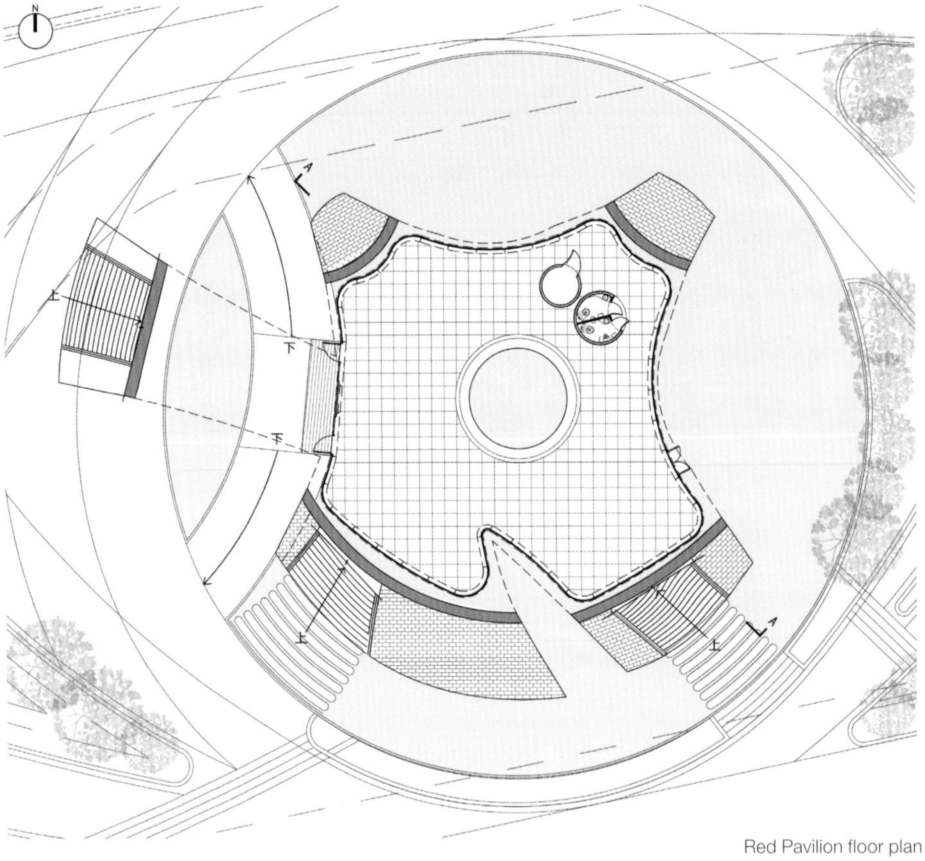

Red Pavilion floor plan

West elevation

North elevation

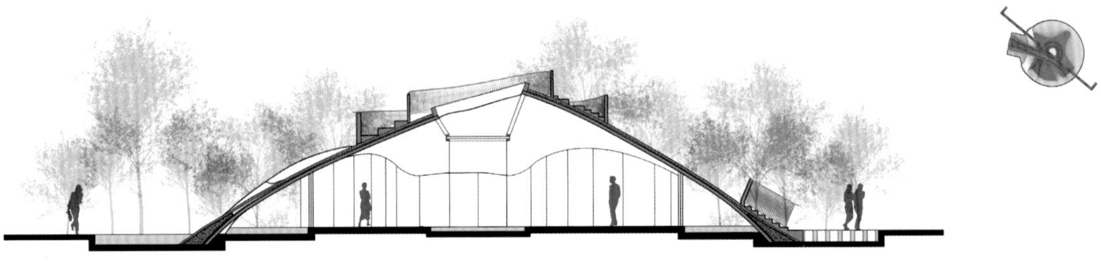

Section A-A

0 1 2 3 4m

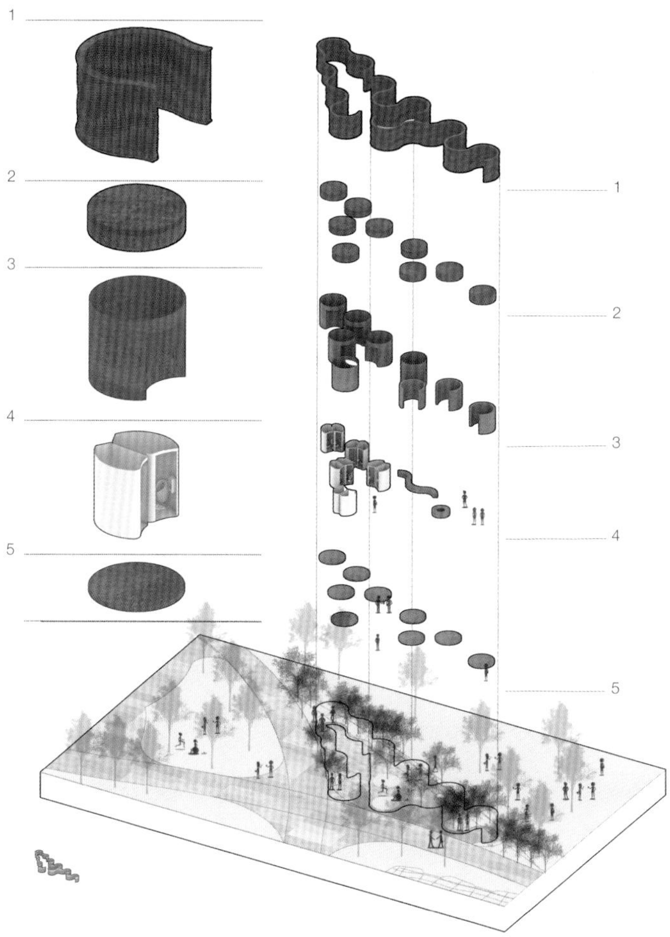

Exploded axonometric diagram of Water Pavilion

1. Parameterized wall
2. Tube roof
3. Outer-tube wall
4. Innter-tube wall and furniture
5. Tube basement

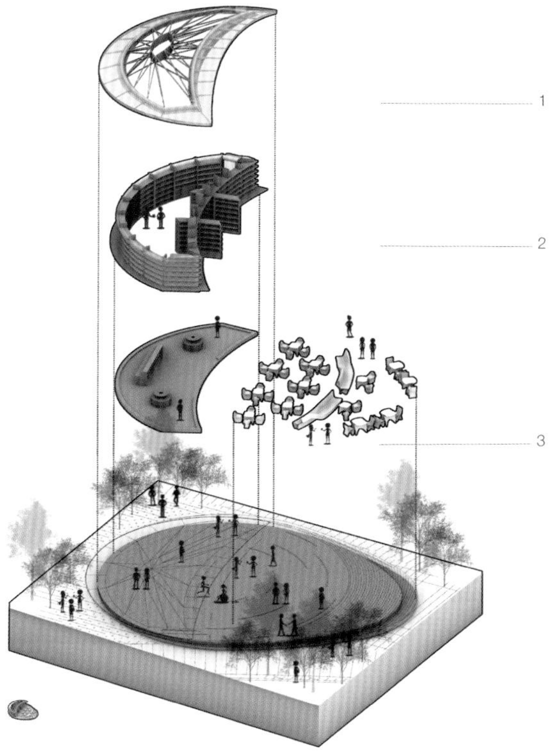

Exploded axonometric diagram of Moon Pavilion

1. Roof
2. Wall
3. Furniture

Exploded axonometric diagram of Red Pavilion

1. Brick
2. Polyurethane insolation
3. Glass fibre isolation layer
4. 3D-printed formwork
5. Stairs
6. Three-layer brick shell structure
7. Insolation system
8. 3D-printed formwork
9. Glass curtain wall

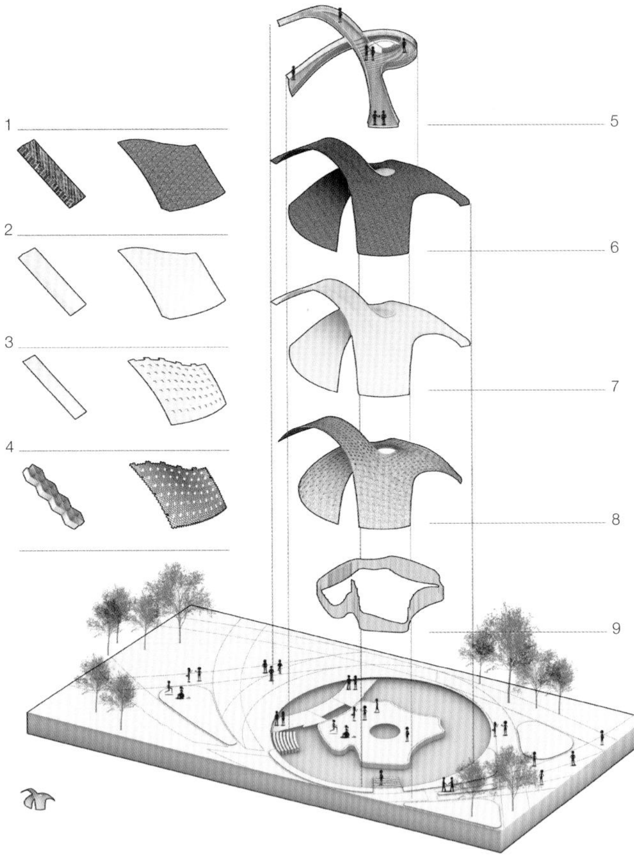

Exploded axonometric diagram of Cloud Pavilion

1. Roof
2. Steel structure
3. Prefabricated 3D-printed façade
4. Glass curtain wall
5. 3D-printed furniture

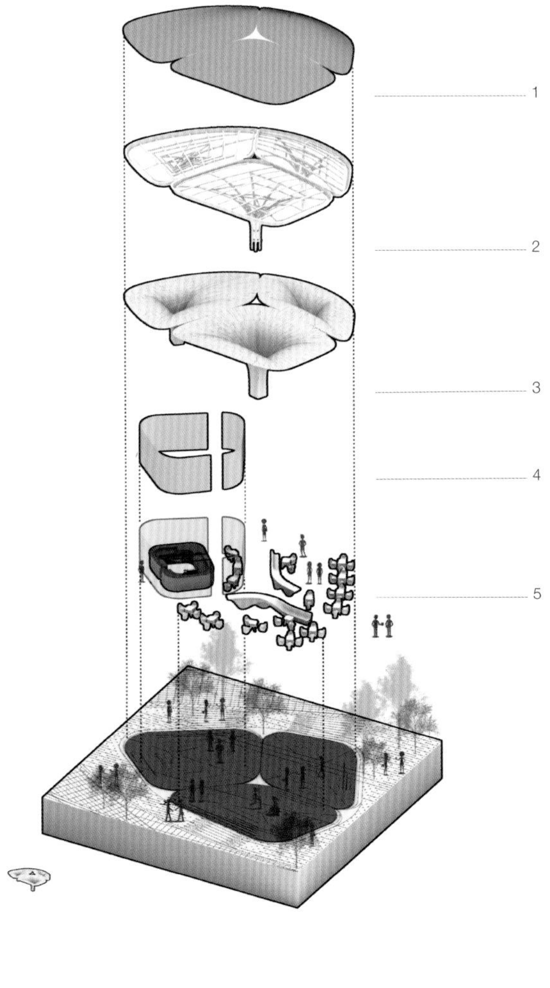

XIAOYUE HOUSE

Rùn Atelier

Location: Shangyu District, Shaoxing, Zhejiang Province
Architect: Rùn Atelier
Principal architect: Wang Hao
Design team: Guo Qi, Li Wei, Zhang Junyu
Area: Site: 514 square meters; floor: 252 square meters
Design period: July 2018–October 2018
Construction period: September 2017–December 2020
Photography: Wu Qingshan

Xiaoyue House is conveniently located within Xiaoyue Park in the Xiaoyue village and neighborhood of Shangyu District in Shaoxing. Newly built small high-rise residences are to the east of the site, and a few old, scattered houses with two or three courtyards are to the west, interspersed with two-story residential houses built along the river system during the 1950s.

A 10-meter-wide river borders the complex's northern wall. A formal entrance gate was placed here at the time of its construction, but the door lintel and stone jambs are rather simple and plain. A more commonly used gate lies to the southern side of the complex. Taking feng shui principles into account, a second door is placed to the left and can be found after entering the southern gate. A 20-meter-tall cedar tree stands in the southern area of the

Xiaoyue House within Xiaoyue Park

View toward courtyard

first courtyard, and a dozen acres of vegetable gardens cover the area across the street from the entrance.

Xiaoyue House features the traditional wooden structure often found in the cities of Ningbo and Shaoxing in the eastern province of Zhejiang. The main building has three rooms, and the whole building complex has three courtyards. Single-story buildings line the east and west sides of the first courtyard and are used as a kitchen and a Buddhist temple respectively. The house at the end of the courtyard has a single-floor three-room layout, with walls that are 3 meters high to the eaves. The pillars of the building are made of local fir. The second courtyard has a two-story main house. One-way staircases are placed to the eastern and western sides, increasing efficiency of movement through the space. The third courtyard, known as Square Garden, is at the northernmost area. The side walls are approximately 10 meters long and it has original Paulownia, Osmanthus, and orange trees.

A village renovation and renewal plan was launched in the Xiaoyue neighborhood in the summer of 2018. The renovation proposal included the dilapidated residential complex, covering a 400-square-meter area. The owner signed a 10-year lease and allowed it to be turned into a small pavilion to display the neighborhood's extensive cultural and architectural history.

View from above

Internal water system connecting the courtyards

Courtyard views

Interior exhibition spaces

Rùn Atelier created an internal water system and planted a spruce tree to transform the building complex into a palace for the tree. This inward-flowing water system connected the courtyards divided by the rows of houses to create an open public space and form a dominant outdoor axis. The original building needed to be distinguished from the village structure so that people from outside could find the inward-oriented residential space. Introducing the outdoor axis changed the original closeness of the complex and formed a new outdoor spatial sequence within the walls. A path zigzags southward from the northern main entrance, passing the through the opened-up space on the second floor and down to the slits in the eaves on the first floor. It then passes through the corridor to the elongated pond to the south, culminating at the cedar tree. The original closed brick walls along the path have been replaced with large areas of transparent glass, providing the main light source for the exhibition halls.

The material palette has been unified indoors and outdoors. The floorboards remained almost intact for hundreds of years. The external and internal walls are made of fermented lime with a slightly treated surface. The external walls were repaired with the original construction technique, thereby integrating the old and the new. The design of the indoor exhibition halls was also unified to match the architectural space.

Elongated pond

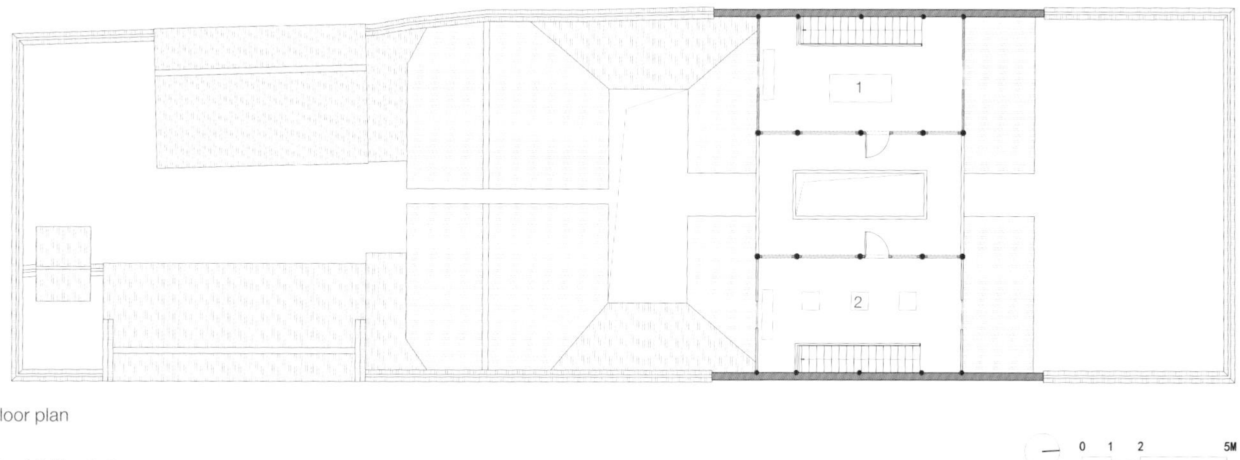

Second-floor plan

1. Folk art exhibition hall
2. Ancient heritage exhibition hall

First-floor plan

1. Intangible cultural heritage exhibition hall
2. Education room
3. Local literati exhibition hall
4. Commerce exhibition hall
5. Folk culture exhibition hall
6. Geography exhibition hall

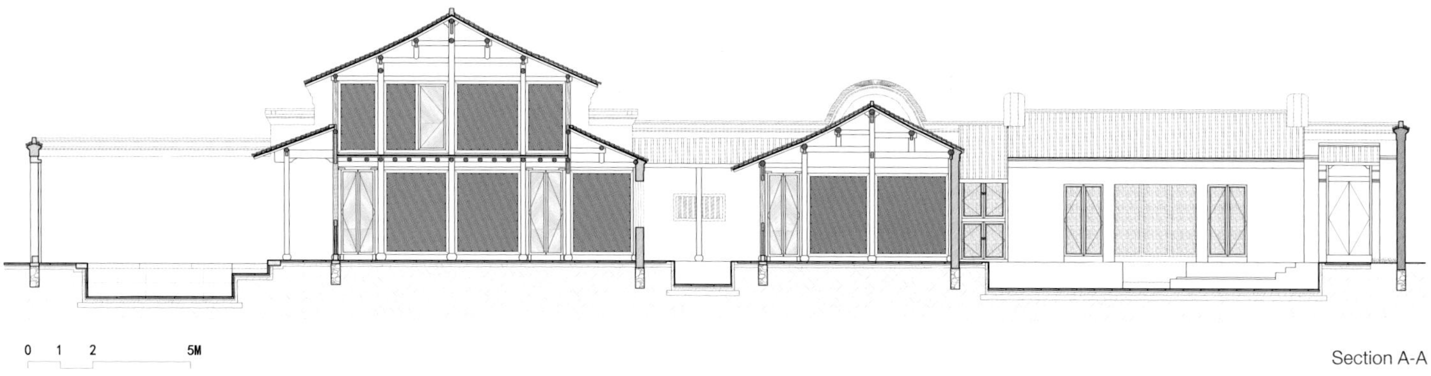

Section A-A

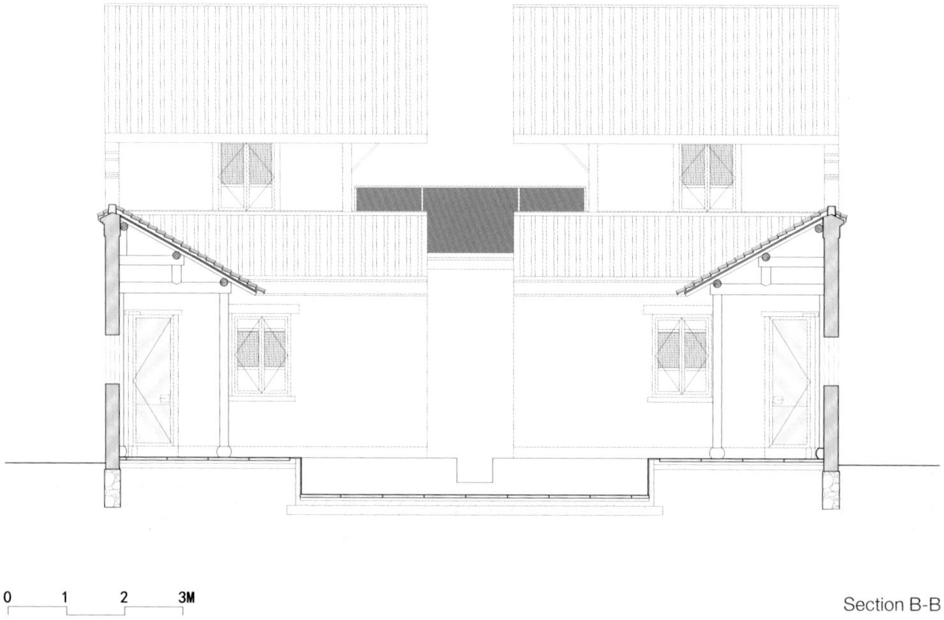

Section B-B

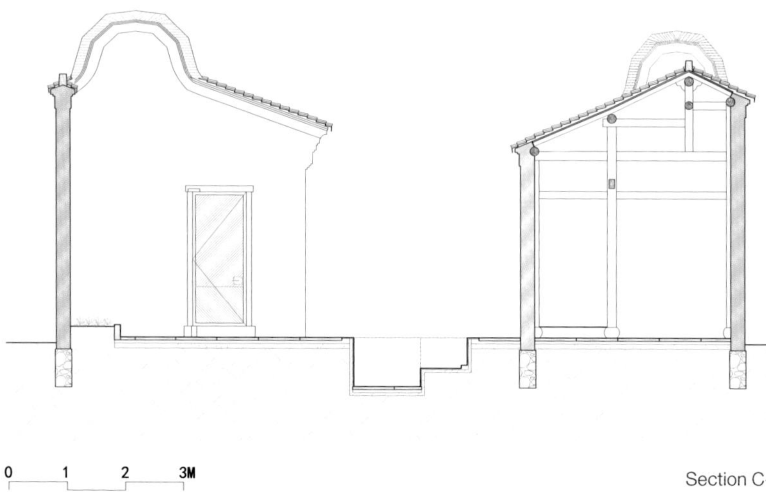

Section C-C

HOUSE CHENG

Rùn Atelier

Location: Biyang Town, Yi County, Huangshang, Anhui Province
Architect: Rùn Atelier
Principal architect: Wang Hao
Design team: Yi Yajie, Li Wei, Chen Siyu, Tang Ming
Area: Site: 1,160 square meters; floor: 811 square meters
Design period: 2016–2019
Construction period: 2017–2020
Photography: Wu Qingshan

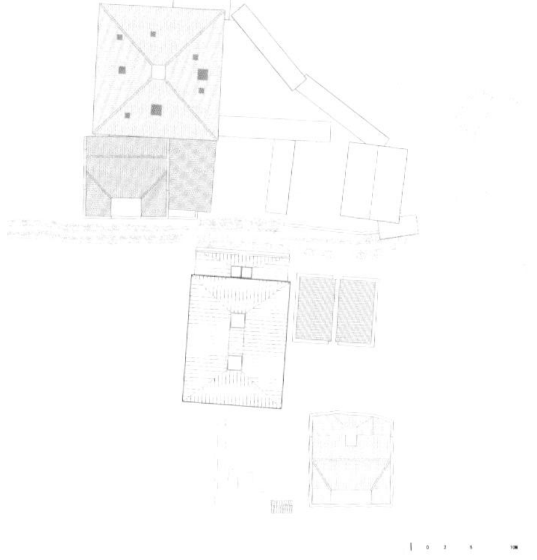

Site plan

Pan Village is located 1 mile from Guanlu Village, Yi County, in the eastern Chinese province of Anhui. The small village is home to 20 to 30 households along a meandering trail through lush paddy fields. Approximately half of the buildings are new, while some of the old houses still have the gray walls typical of traditional local homes built after the late Qing dynasty. The client is a fan of Argentinian writer Jorge Luis Borges and wanted to create a "garden of forking paths," which is the title of a short story written by Borges in 1941.

The 2,500-square-meter site is located at the edge of the village. It contained a few dilapidated structures, with the ancestral temple of Pan Village being the most important one. However, it had been converted into housing for production teams during the Cultural Revolution. The elegant wooden frame of the temple had disappeared much earlier,

Aerial view of Pan Village

House Cheng under construction

replaced by a simple timber frame. Yet, the front gate had been preserved. The exquisite wax-gourd beams imitating stone and the brick carvings showcase how important the building used to be. Several other ruins only retain their gray-brick rowlock walls, less than one-story high. The owner spent a lot of time and energy acquiring these houses with the plan to rebuild a new village surrounded by fields.

Architect Wang Hao was attracted to the chaotic layout of ruins and the mix of old and new houses. The village didn't carry the heavy historical burden typical of some older villages, which means it could become an ideal example of contemporary village renewal. It is also a place where the surrounding terrain and fields are extremely ordinary with no significant geographical characteristics within close proximity.

Scene of contruction

Gate detail

During construction

Interior view of House Cheng under construction

During construction

Rùn Atelier employed a richer diversity of construction materials and methods than was already evident in this ordinary Huizhou village. Different wooden structures, according to function, are arranged within the walls demarcated by the ruins. The new wooden structures are derived from traditional mortise and tenon joints to create this diversity. They represent a set of established styles developed by Rùn Atelier during recent years, but that still needed to overcome difficulties in the face of actual construction. A group of carpenters from neighboring Zhejiang Province improved and corrected the mortise and tenon joints that were not feasible in the original design.

The woodcraft construction included three types of wooden structures. First, a traditional *chuan-dou*-style wooden structure. Second, a newly created mortise-and-tenon wooden structure called "bundled column with stacked beams." Third, a steel-and-wood structure that combined modern European and American wooden structure techniques. Artisans made use of their wisdom and techniques in these different structure types to create a landscape of diverse crafts.

House Cheng is expected to be completed in 2020, restoring the diversity at the nearly abandoned edge of Pan Village. Incorporating the important woodcrafts that remain in the countryside, it will bridge the gap between craft and design, yet still be hidden within the high enclosed walls.

Second-floor plan

First-floor plan

1. House I
2. Lobby
3. House II
4. House III
5. House IV
6. Cafeteria
7. Reception
8. Tea house
9. Lotus pond
10. Equipment room
11. Private courtyard
12. Rice field landscape
13. Water pond

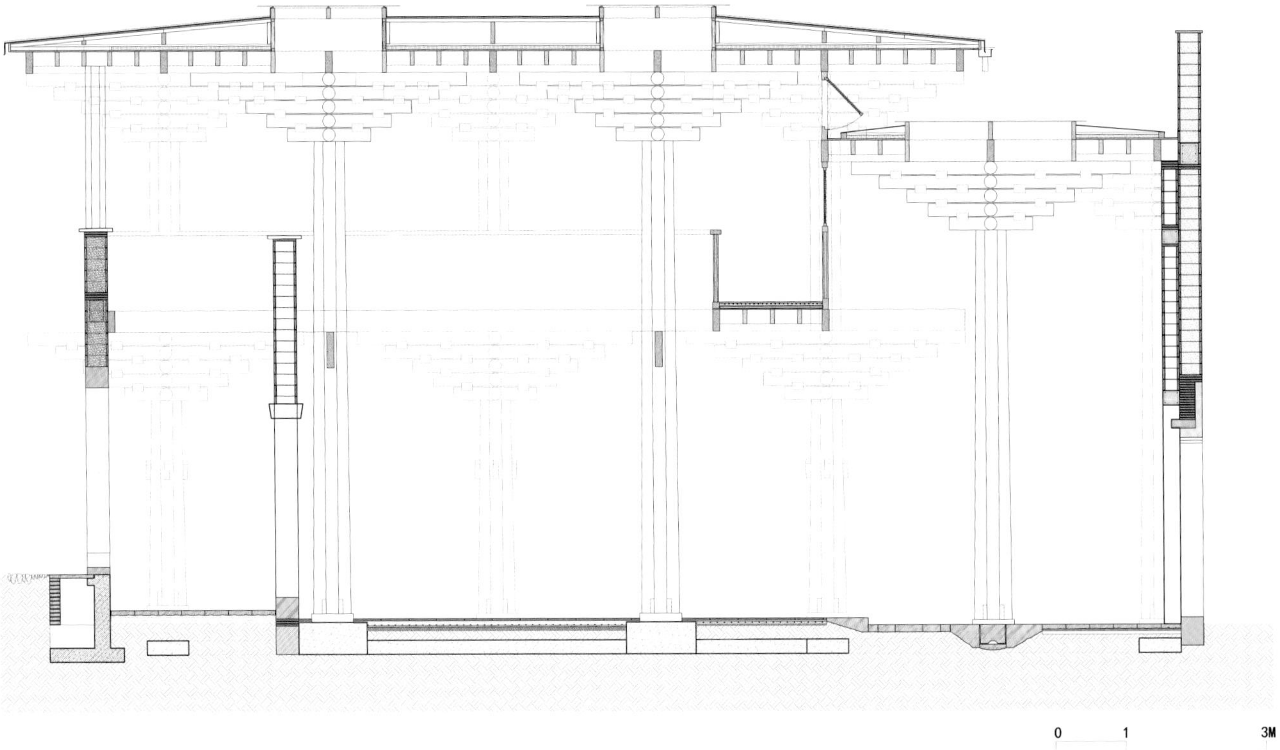

Section A-A

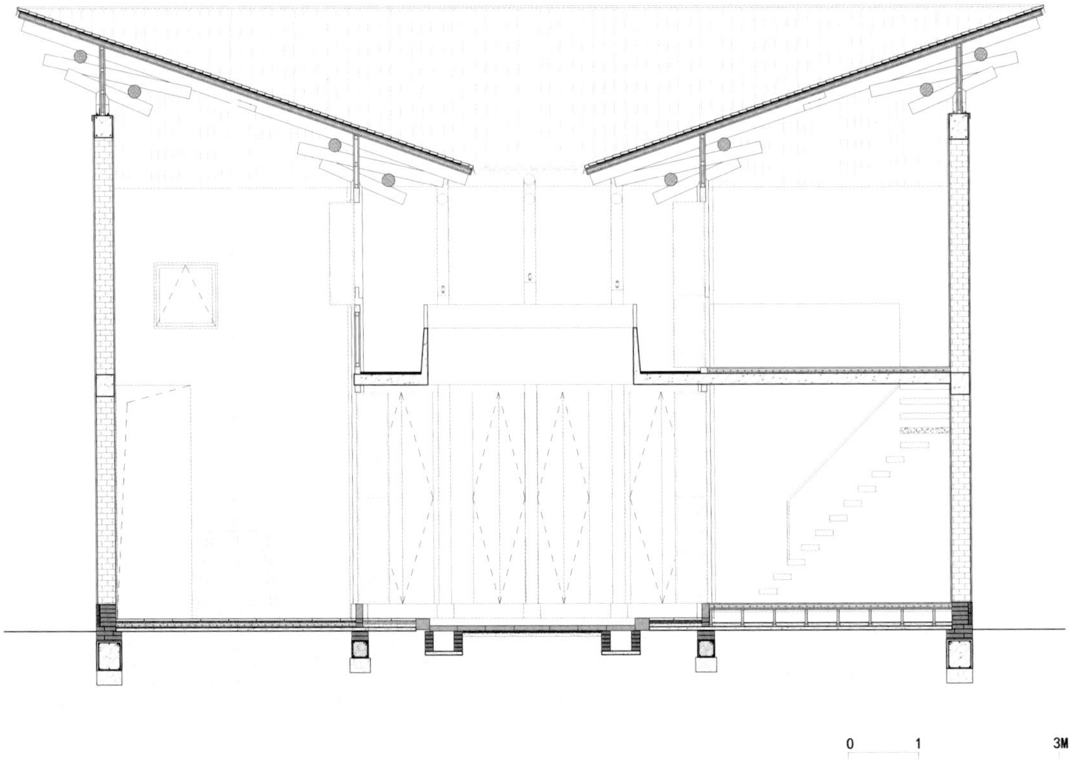

Section B-B

JINXIAN RIVER PUBLIC SPACE NODES

SWArchitects

Location: Linyi City, Shandong Province
Architect: SWArchitects
Principal architects: Song Wei, Tian Weijia
Design team: Sun Xun, Zhong Kaiqiang, Sun Wanyi, Wang Yiran, Hao Xiangnan
Area: 5,500 square meters
Project completion: November 2018
Photography: Yu Weimin

Site plan

More than a dozen original villages line Jinxian River, which is located in the Mengshan Scenic Region of Linyi City, Shandong Province. The design of the public space nodes along this river is an evolving project, which includes a new riverside pedestrian walkway and enlarged public spaces. The functional positioning of the amplified nodes varies according to the needs of the villagers' daily life and the operational requirements of the scenic spots.

Paving filled with red haws creates a continuous line through the landscape

The newly built Hawthorn Square continues the original function of the site, which villagers used to collect and dry their haws. It is paved with stones of different textures, creating lines that divide up the square. The change in pattern is further enhanced by several wide, straight lines. The paving filled with red haws and the walkway along Jinxian River form a continuous red landscape belt when viewed from above.

A large open space on the scale of Hawthorn Square is a precious natural resource in this mountainous area. A small drop separates the higher temporary parking lot at street level from the open square by the water below. The two levels are connected by wedge-shaped stairs, which are cut into their triangular shape by the paved slope for barrier-free access. Due to the limitations of the construction process and engineering difficulties in the mountains, treated wood replaces the sharp angles of the stone slabs of the steps. The juxtaposition of the two materials emphasizes the geometry of the interlacing pavement lines. The stonework pattern, with its separation lines, echoes the shape of the farmland opposite the motorway, embodying the contemporary concept of building with nature. The patches of different paving materials surround the original site's hawthorn trees, while stone benches are arranged around the rectangular tree groups, in order to provide sufficient resting space for villagers. They often sit on these benches and chat while their haws dry in the sun.

Landscape detail

Bird's-eye view of Hawthorn Square

Hawthorn Square is paved with stones of different textures

Stairs connect the higher temporary parking lot at street level from the open square by the water below

Treated wood replaces the sharp angles of the stone steps

Pavement detail

Aerial view of Fountain Square

Pavements of Fountain Square

Fountain Square is located next to a small dam that widens Jinxian River, and is named after the circular fountain of the square. The square has sections of differing elevations and uses retaining walls to divide the square into platforms along its long axis.

The square is divided into three platforms. The upper level is made of hard pavement and contains a central fountain. Unlike traditional square designs, where the water feature is placed on a low level, this project puts the central water feature on an elevation to take advantage of the dynamic fountain landscape and guide pedestrians to the inner parts of the square. The middle area is made up of the original water dam spillway and maintains the original vegetation formed by the humid waterway. It also features elongated blocks for people to rest on both sides of the waterway. The lower part of the square is composed of the parking area trees. The meticulous geometric placement of the trees contrasts the texture of the mountain vegetation behind and echoes the pavement topography.

With the premise of maintaining basic functions and traditional stone elements, SWArchitects advanced the design of the Jinxian River public space nodes to create a balance between tradition and modernity.

Plan of Hawthorn Square

Plan of Fountain Square

SPRING GARDEN

Architects & Engineers Co., Ltd, Southeast University

Location: Dingshu Town, Yixing City, Jiangsu Province
Architect: Architects & Engineers Co., Ltd, Southeast University
Principal architect: Ge Ming
Design team: Ji Hongliang, Chen Jieping, Kong Yiming, Liu Xiaodan, Wang Zhengxin
Structural design: Chun Qing
Area: Site: 25,665 square meters; floor: 437 square meters
Design period: 2015
Project completion: 2018
Photography: Chen Hao, Jiang Mengling, Han Siyuan

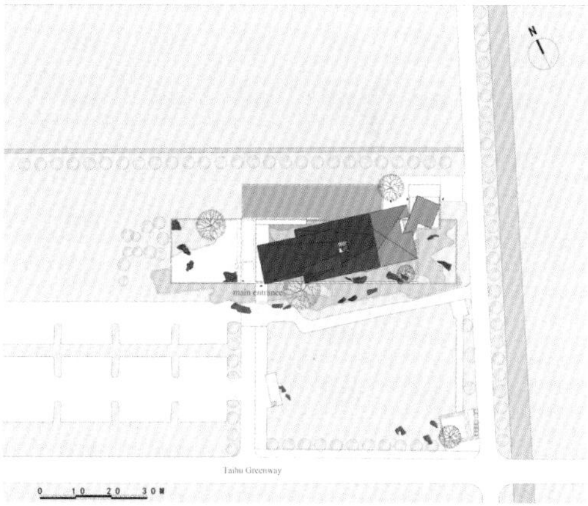

Site plan

Since 2014, architect Ge Ming has designed a batch of small public buildings and facilities near Taihu Lake in the suburbs of Dingshu Town, Yixing City. Called "Three Gardens and One Market," they consist of a Spring Garden, Autumn Garden, Winter Garden, and Summer Market. The ongoing project prompted Ge Ming to gain a new understanding of the uniqueness of landscaping methods and their relationship with other design techniques. Among the gardens, Spring Garden functions as a visitor center with parking spaces for bicycles, while also marking the starting point and resting place for the Taihu Greenway Bicycle Race.

West elevation

South elevation

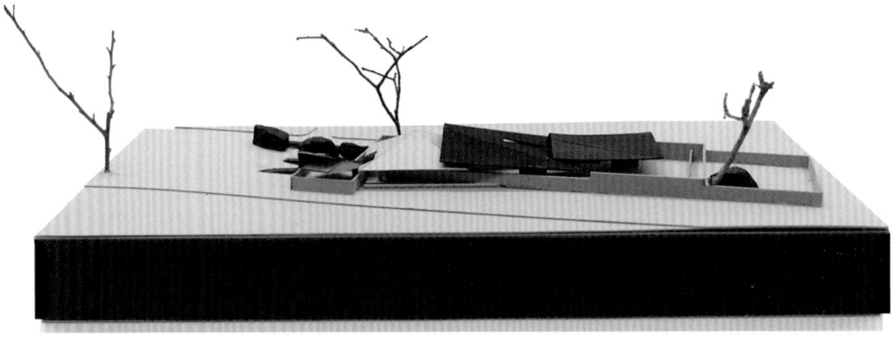

Architectural model

Ge Ming adopted a "half garden-half house" design in response to the narrow, elongated site. As such, part of the garden is inside the house, and part of the house is in the garden. Thereby, the structure can be both extended and rotated accordingly.

In terms of the methods employed, he used structure and plot division simultaneously. Firstly, four slanted roofs form a group of compound slopes that overlap each other and form a series of overlays and in-between spaces, resulting in a special structure on the site. Secondly, the plot is divided. The areas of land and water, such as pools, islands, platforms, and pits, are intertwined to correspond with the compounded roof slopes and thus complete the construction of the half garden-half house. The remaining service facilities and parking spaces take the shape of folded edges wedged into the building and connected to the compound slope roof, water stones, and terraces.

The concept of "articulation" was introduced during construction in order to advance the landscaping techniques. The concept focuses on forming a succession between nature and man-made objects, making it necessary to create transitional gaps. For this reason, a specific sloping method is used in Spring Garden to form segments. The roof covers areas of land and water, but its contact points are hidden in the shadow between the slopes and appear only in reflections on the water, which effectively segments the site while also providing an opportunity for the shadows and gaps to act as connections.

Great importance was attached to the creation of an airy atmosphere in Spring Garden, to fully express the importance of both a travelling mind and a meditative state. It is named Spring Garden because it adopts a half garden-half house structure and uses a compound slope to express the image of "hidden spring," implying potential vitality.

Moss garden beneath overlapping roofs

Moss garden details

Sand garden

Interior of the covered atrium

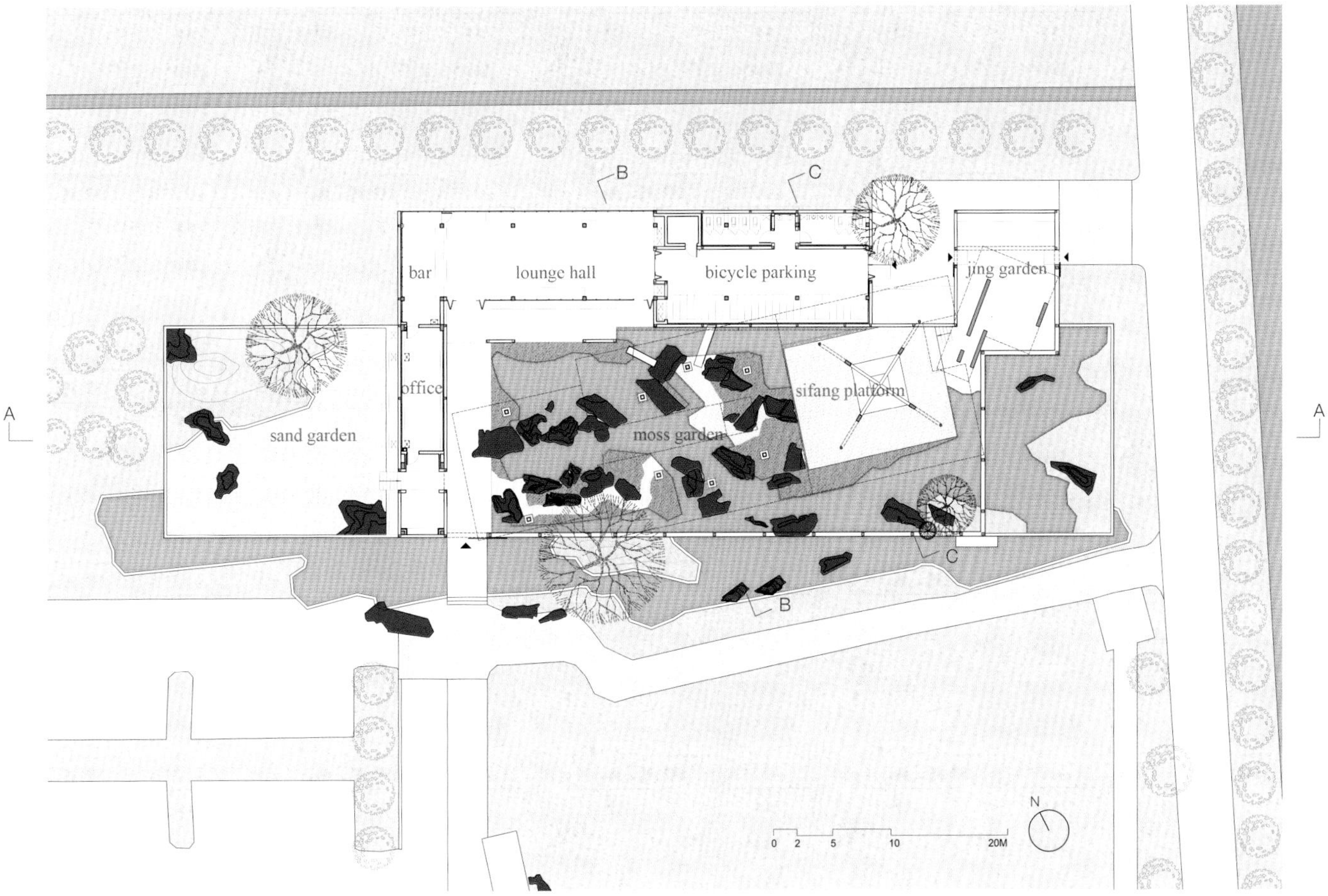

First-floor plan

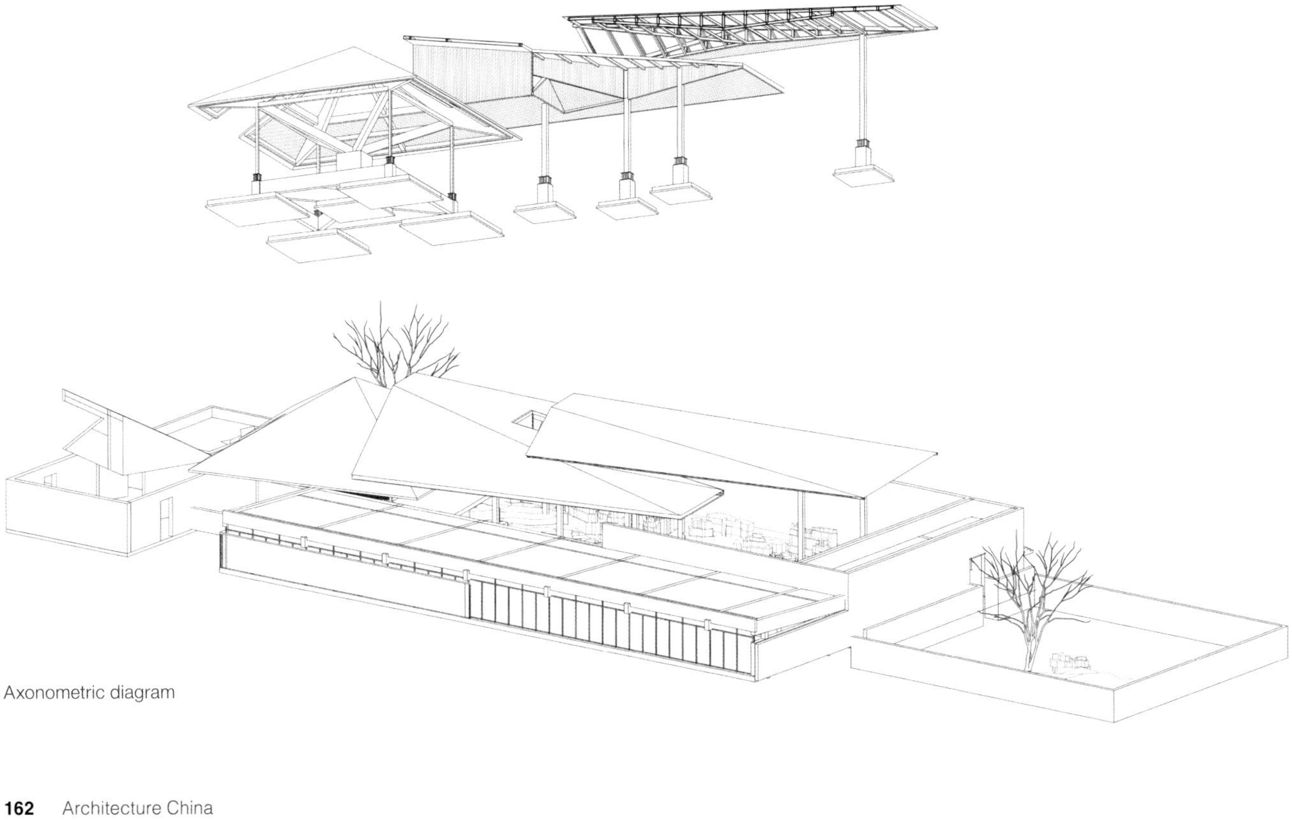

Axonometric diagram

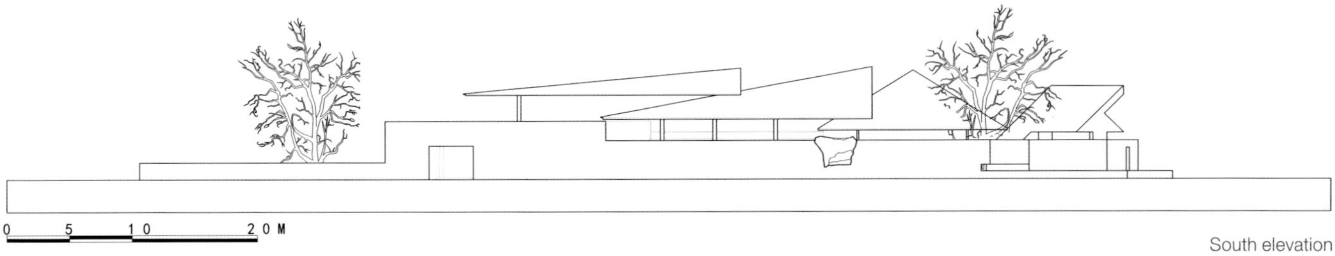

South elevation

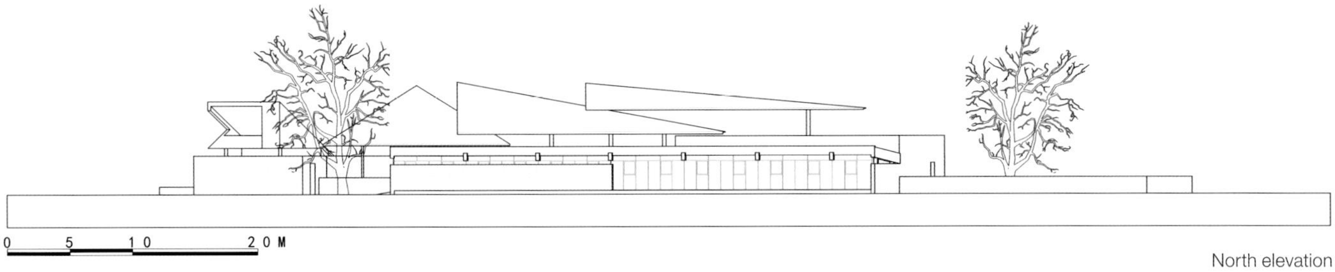

North elevation

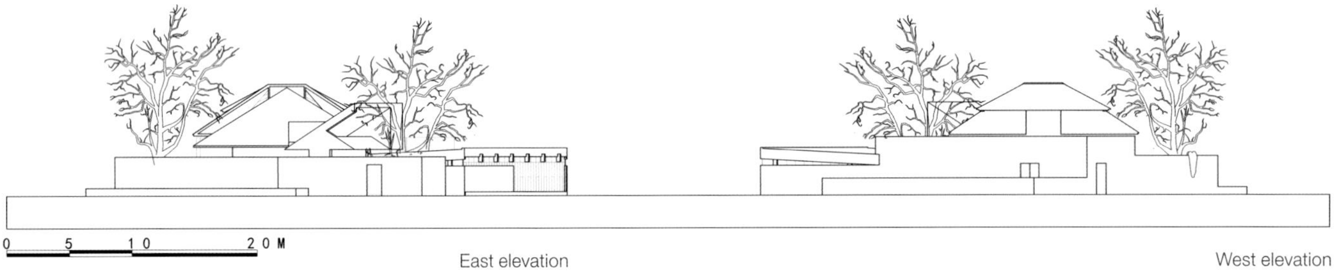

East elevation

West elevation

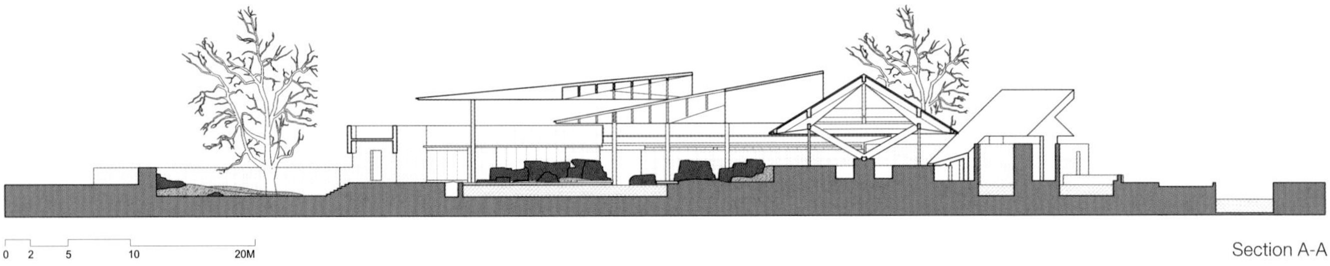

Section A-A

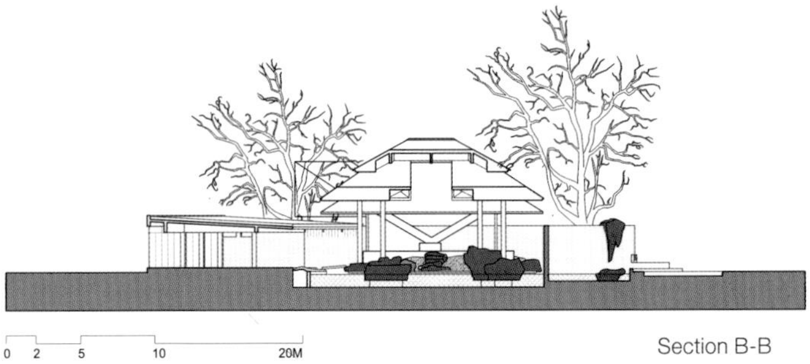

Section B-B

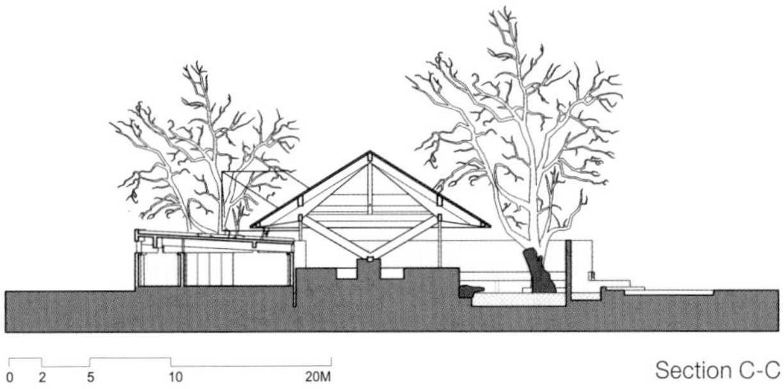

Section C-C

TERRA RETREAT BOUTIQUE HOTEL

Duoxiang Studio

Location: Dawan Village, Zhongwei, Ningxia Hui Autonomous Region
Architect: Duoxiang Studio
Principal architect: Jia Lianna
Design team: Bai Chen, Xiao Yuqin, Zhou Chen, Lin Weicheng, Cui Lan, Sun Xueyi, Zhao Ni
Structural design: Liu Su
Area: Site: 3,022 square meters; floor: 1,164 square meters
Design period: August 2017–February 2019
Construction period: November 2017–April 2019

Site plan

The site is located in the Shapotou District of Zhongwei City in the Ningxia Hui Autonomous Region. Yellow River turns 180 degrees to form a horseshoe-shaped oasis named Dawan Village, which translates to "big bend." Positioned in the southwest of this oasis, the site for Terra Retreat Boutique Hotel is a truly unique landscape, featuring a small forest to the west, and the desert beyond Yellow River.

The first planning stages of the project began with how to balance the solid mass of the buildings and the emptiness of the courtyards. During initial on-site inspections, the southwestern corner, home to an apricot tree and a few walnut trees, stood out to the architects as being very impressive. They immediately felt the welcoming atmosphere and a sense of belonging, and wanted to retain this powerful experience in the design.

View across rooftops

Central courtyard

The apricot tree is the entrance point to the hotel village. Six buildings, including four guest buildings, a village kitchen, and an administration office, surround a central courtyard to create a village-like layout. Two buildings, A1 and B1, are to the west of the site. They are built on top of an existing foundation and have views of the forest and Yellow River. Two guest rooms, A2 and C2, are to the north and south of the site respectively. Due to a blocked horizontal view and unfavorable landscape conditions to the east, the ground level of building B3 was raised to guide the line of sight upward. For the same reasons, the interior layout also adopts a vertical development strategy with the installation of a loft and terrace to provide different experiences. The small A3 building, serving as the hotel office, is located in the northeastern corner of the site. It retains the original layout's foundation and the original trees of the site.

Different activity spaces are created in the central courtyard through the combination of platforms with varying elevations, different building materials, and terraces and surrounding walls of different heights. These include spaces to bask in the sun, to rest in the shade, and to sit around a fireplace. A castle staircase leads up to the public roof terrace, and forms a yin and yang relationship with the large open courtyard. Several interesting loops cater for children playing games. The large fireplace in the central courtyard and smaller fireplace facing the forest provide two spaces for keeping warm and taking in the scenery.

The kitchen at the village entrance is an important place for arrivals and departures. It is located under the eaves of the building's southern and eastern walls, providing a proper welcome and shelter. All guest rooms are accessed via the central courtyard, and the access to each guesthouse is distinct and captures its unique relationship with the site.

The main body of the building is a concrete frame with a partially wooden structure. As the civil works of the site were constructed ahead of time, some of the architect's decisions were made before the indoor layout was fully determined. They retained some flexibility in the positioning of skylights and wall openings, which also created challenges and unexpected solutions for the subsequent detailed design of the interior space. Wooden framework porches—an important local architectural element in the traditional dwellings of Zhongwei City—are integrated into spaces beneath eaves or semi-outdoor transitional spaces.

Guest rooms are accessed via the central courtyard

Night scenes

The main body of the building is a concrete frame with a partially wooden structure

Walls of different heights

Guesthouse interiors

Guesthouse interiors

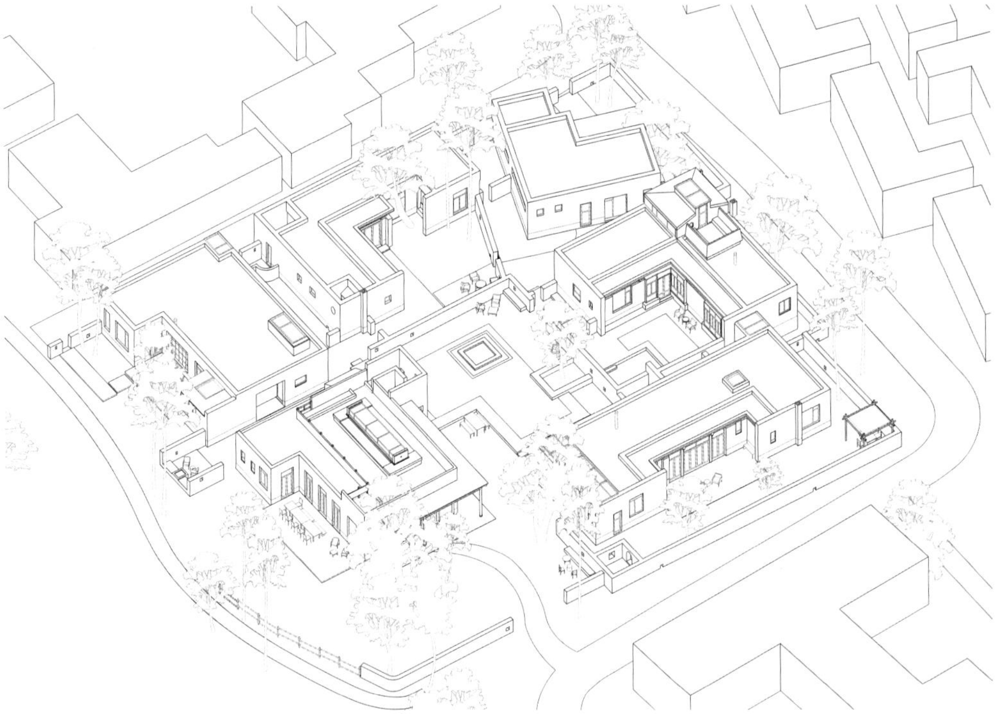

Axonometric drawing

First-floor plan

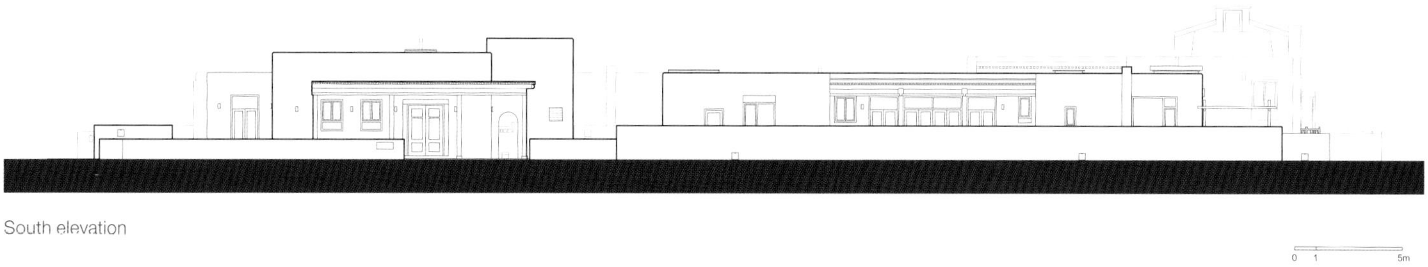

South elevation

North elevation

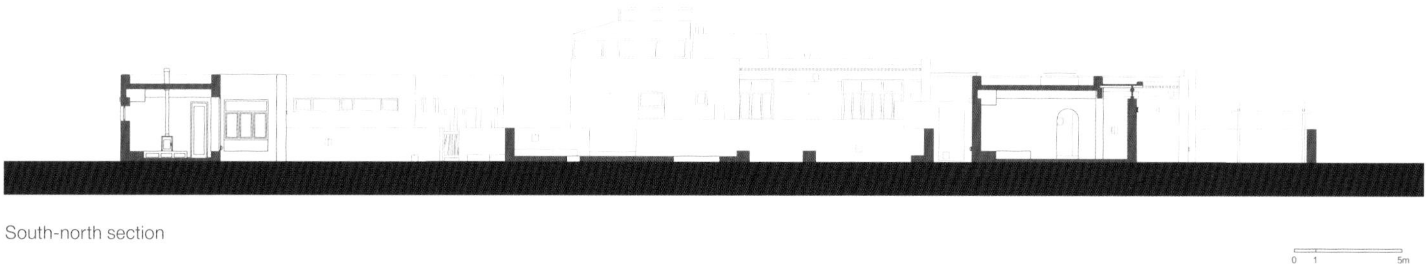

South-north section

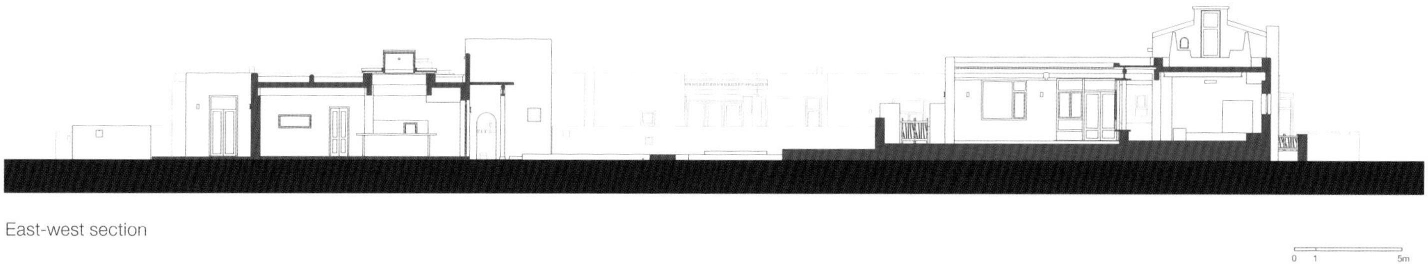

East-west section

Construction details

1. Cement cover
2. Reinforced-concrete coping
3. Pine wood panel
4. Pine wood purlin
5. Pine wood beam
6. Wood beam
7. Aluminum alloy window frame
8. Reinforced-concrete window sill
9. Plaster layer
10. Firebrick layer
11. Gravel layer
12. Reinforced-concrete structure

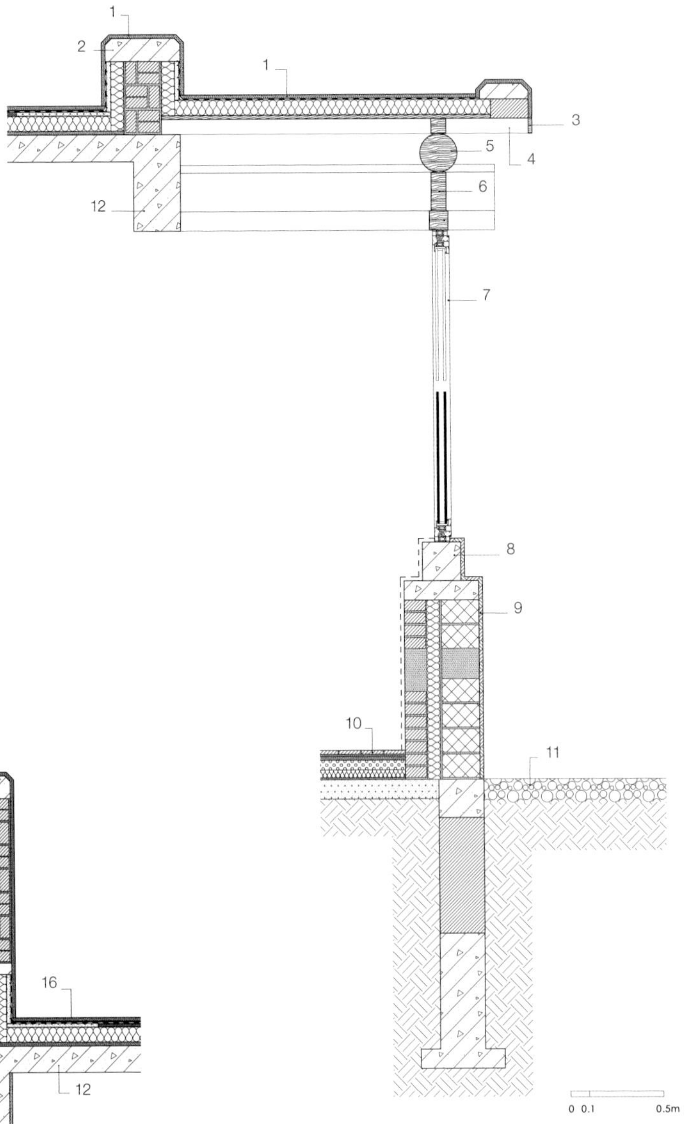

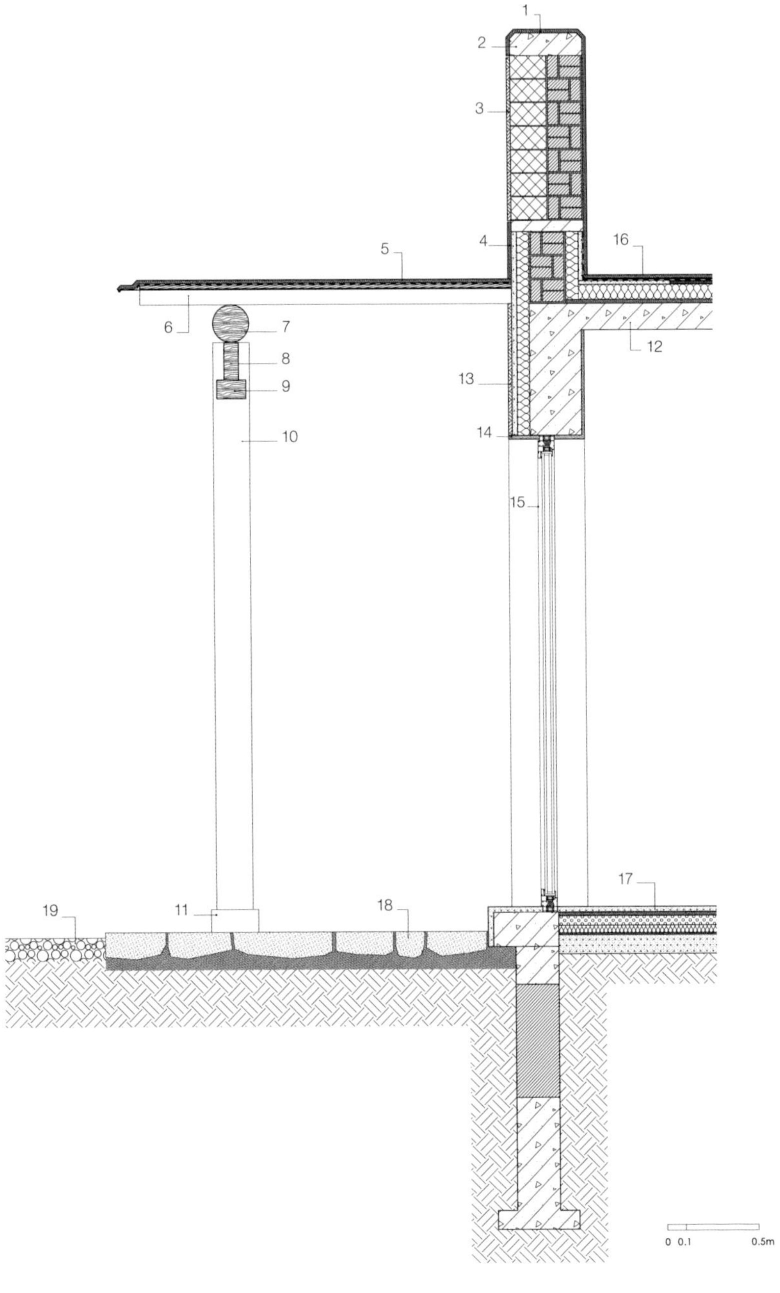

Construction details

1. Cement cover
2. Reinforced-concrete coping
3. Mortar layer
4. Cement cover
5. Protective layer of cement
6. Pine wood purlin
7. Pine wood beam
8. Pine wood beam
9. Wood beam
10. Wood beam
11. Stone base
12. Reinforced-concrete structure
13. Mortar layer
14. Cement cover
15. Aluminum alloy door frame
16. Protective layer of cement
17. Cement cover
18. Rubble layer
19. Gravel layer